The Little Book
of
SAYINGS OF
OSCAR WILDE

The Little Book

of

SAYINGS OF
OSCAR WILDE

Edited by

ALEXANDER NOBLE

p

This is a Parragon Book

This edition published in 2000

Parragon
Queen Street House
4 Queen Street
Bath BA1 1HE, UK

Produced by Magpie Books, an imprint of
Robinson Publishing Ltd, London

ISBN 0-75253-173-5

A copy of the British Library Cataloguing-in-Publication Data
is available from the British Library
Printed in China

Contents

Introduction 6

Introduction

Oscar Wilde is rightly renowned for his epigrams. Many, in original form, such as "Work is the curse of the drinking classes" or "The unspeakable in full pursuit of the inedible," have passed into the common coinage of the English language.

Wilde liked to think of himself as an antinomian, one who believes that dualities exist, that two contradictory statements can both be true, and that paradoxes are plausible. His writings take many forms: a novel, several light-hearted short stories, dramas, poetry, essays and letters. The plays are still put on, and the novel is available in high-street bookstores. These two aspects of his writing create the popular impression of Wilde: the doyen of the world of high society – a world of gilded indolence and cynical wit – an aesthete, a languorous flower casually passing his observations on life. In fact he was much more rounded than that. In plays such as A Woman of No Importance and An Ideal Husband there is a darker undercurrent: in the former the cruelty of a cynical philanderer and in the latter the revelation that a good man's whole career has been based on an immoral act. Lady Windermere's Fan is a comedy of errors but only barely — with but the most minor twist to the plot it could have been a tragedy of errors.

Wilde took the ideas of Aestheticism seriously. He was greatly influenced by Pater and Ruskin, and he sincerely felt that genuine art is its own justification. He went beyond Aestheticism in later life as it became clear to him that art and beauty are not in themselves sufficient for life and that love, sorrow and other emotions have their place. His flamboyant and dandified clothing was an assertion of his independence of convention, which in his era was particularly uniform regarding dress.

Wilde had many other concerns. His mother was keen to see Ireland independent, and Wilde inherited her views. Despite the popular conception of him as revolving in super-English high society, he was not very keen on Englishness, as occasionally slips out in his plays and is more obvious in his philosophical essays The Soul of

Man under Socialism *and* The Decay of Lying. *He also thought of himself as a socialist and as an anarchist. His socialism was somewhat Utopian, being based on the idea that there was sufficient wealth in the UK, if distributed evenly, to expand greatly the leisure of the working man and essentially free his creative spirit. He had no truck with the idea of the dignity of labor, much preferring the idea of the indignity of machines. The freeing of the working man from degrading physical work he thought would lead to a broader Individualism (of a beneficent, benevolent kind). His anarchy was fairly literal – to be free of rules and laws and conventions.*

Convicted of gross indecency after losing a libel case, Wilde spent two years in prison from 1895 to 1897. From this emerged De Profundis, *in which he came to terms with his great disgrace and developed a much more humble philosophy of life. It was written for Lord Alfred Douglas, who had originally egged Wilde on in suing Douglas's father, the Marquess of Queensberry, for defamation. Although patchy (in that it covers a wide variety of topics, including Douglas's destruction of Wilde as artist and person) it shows that Wilde's capacity for original thought was not totally dimmed.*

Wilde's originality, his use of wit, the paradox and the unexpected, and his accurate observations, put the needle into the balloon of late Victorian English complacency, with its illiberality, its conformism and its hypocrisy. Given that these qualities still exist in society, much of his writing is as valid today as when it was written.

Chapter 1

IRONIES AND PARADOXES

Much of Wilde's impact comes from his ability to turn a common saying on its head. His capacity to come up consistently with the unexpected leads his audience at first to laughter and then often to thought. Frequently, there is a message in the jokes, and one should not be taken in by their outward lightness or profusion.

Wilde's witticisms are not always consistent with each other. Many of his sayings come in fact from the mouths of his characters. Thus we have the extreme cynicism of Lord Henry Wotton in The Picture of Dorian Gray or of Lord Illingworth in A Woman of No Importance, both dubious characters. And even the essay "The Decay of Lying" takes the form of a dialogue between two fictional characters, which allows the author to take a more rarefied position than his own might have been.

Divorces are made in Heaven ...

The Importance of Being Earnest

I can resist everything except temptation.

Lady Windermere's Fan

The English country gentleman galloping after a fox
— the unspeakable in full pursuit of the inedible.

A Woman of No Importance

I choose my friends for their good looks, my acquain-
tances for their good characters, and my enemies for
their good intellects. A man cannot be too careful in
the choice of his enemies!

The Picture of Dorian Gray

I can stand brute force, but brute reason is quite unbearable. There is something unfair about its use. It is hitting below the intellect.

The Picture of Dorian Gray

… remain, as I do, incomprehensible: to be great is to be misunderstood.

Letters

… if a man knows the law there is nothing illegal he cannot do when he likes: that is why folk become lawyers. That is about all they are good for.

Vera, or the Nihilists

… there is only one thing in the world worse than being talked about, and that is not being talked about.

The Picture of Dorian Gray

I dislike arguments of any kind. They are always vulgar, and often convincing.

The Importance of Being Earnest

… I think that life is far too important a thing to talk seriously about it.

Lady Windermere's Fan

Nowadays people know the price of everything and the value of nothing.

The Picture of Dorian Gray

Nowadays people know the price of everything and the value of nothing.

When one is in love, one always begins by deceiving one's self, and one always ends by deceiving others.

The Picture of Dorian Gray

Children begin by loving their parents; as they grow older they judge them; sometimes they forgive them.

The Picture of Dorian Gray

I love acting. It is so much more real than life.

The Picture of Dorian Gray

The fact is that the public have an insatiable curiosity to know everything, except what is worth knowing.

The Soul of Man under Socialism

… hard work is simply the refuge of people who have nothing whatever to do.

The Remarkable Rocket

When one is in town one amuses oneself. When one is in the country one amuses other people. It is excessively boring.

The Importance of Being Earnest

Moderation is a fatal thing … Nothing succeeds like excess.

A Woman of No Importance

Wickedness is a myth invented by good people to account for the curious attractiveness of others.

"Phrases and Philosophies for the Use of the Young"

To love oneself is the beginning of a life-long romance.

"Phrases and Philosophies for the Use of the Young"

For the aim of the liar is simply to charm, to delight, to give pleasure. He is the very basis of civilized society.

The Decay of Lying

Truth is entirely and absolutely a matter of style.

The Decay of Lying

... it is absurd to have a hard and fast rule about what one should read and what one shouldn't. More than half of modern culture depends on what one shouldn't read.

The Importance of Being Earnest

... land has ceased to be either a profit or a pleasure. It gives one position, and prevents one from keeping it up.

The Importance of Being Earnest

Relations are simply a tedious pack of people, who haven't the remotest knowledge of how to live, nor the smallest instinct about when to die.

The Importance of Being Earnest

Musical people are so absurdly unreasonable. They always want one to be perfectly dumb at the very moment when one is longing to be absolutely deaf.

An Ideal Husband

On peut adorer une langue sans bien la parler, comme on peut aimer une femme sans la connaître. [One can adore a language without speaking it well, just as one can love a woman without knowing her.]

Letters

Cultivated idleness seems to me to be the proper occupation for man.

Letters

... a sentimentalist is simply one who desires to have the luxury of an emotion without paying for it.

Letters

The opinions of the old on matters of Art are, of course, of no value whatsoever. The artistic instincts of the young are invariably fascinating ...

Letters

Between me and life there is a mist of words always. I throw probability out of the window for the sake of a phrase, and the chance of an epigram makes me desert truth.

Letters

One is sure to be disappointed if one tries to get romance out of modern life.

Vera, or the Nihilists

I thought life was going to be a brilliant comedy ... I found it to be a revolting and repellent tragedy ...

Letters

~·&·~

Even the finest and the most self-sacrificing emotions have to be paid for. Strangely enough, that is what makes them fine. The intellectual and emotional life of ordinary people is a very contemptible affair. Just as they borrow their ideas from a sort of circulating library of thought ... and send them back soiled at the end of each week, so they always try to get their emotions on credit, and refuse to pay the bill when it comes in.

Letters

~·&·~

As soon as you have to pay for an emotion you will know its quality, and be the better for such knowledge. And remember that the sentimentalist is always a cynic at heart. Indeed sentimentality is merely the bank holiday of cynicism.

Letters

The Academy is too large and too vulgar. Whenever I have gone there, there have been either so many people that I have not been able to see the pictures, which was dreadful, or so many pictures that I have not been able to see the people, which was worse.

The Picture of Dorian Gray

But beauty, real beauty, ends where an intellectual expression begins. Intellect is in itself a mode of exaggeration, and destroys the harmony of any face. The moment one sits down to think, one becomes all nose, or all forehead, or something horrid. Look at the successful men in any of the learned professions. How perfectly hideous they are! Except, of course, in the Church. But then in the Church they don't think.

The Picture of Dorian Gray

I have grown to love secrecy. It seems to be the one thing that can make modern life mysterious or marvellous to us. The commonest thing is delightful if only one hides it.

The Picture of Dorian Gray

I quite sympathise with the rage of the English democracy against what they call the vices of the upper orders. The masses feel that drunkenness, stupidity, and immorality should be their own special property, and that if any one of us makes an ass of himself he is poaching on their preserves.

The Picture of Dorian Gray

Poets are not so scrupulous as you are. They know how useful passion is for publication. Nowadays a broken heart will run to many editions.

The Picture of Dorian Gray

It is a sad thing to think of, but there is no doubt that Genius lasts longer than Beauty. That accounts for the fact that we all take such pains to over-educate ourselves. In the wild struggle for existence, we want to have something that endures, and so we fill our minds with rubbish and facts, in the silly hope of keeping our place ... The mind of the thoroughly well-informed man is a dreadful thing. It is like a bric-à-brac shop, all monsters and dust, with everything priced above its proper value.

The Picture of Dorian Gray

Those who are faithful know only the trivial side of love: it is the faithless who know love's tragedies.

The Picture of Dorian Gray

We degenerate into hideous puppets, haunted by the memory of the passions of which we were too much afraid, and the exquisite temptations that we had not the courage to yield to. Youth! Youth! There is absolutely nothing in the world but youth!

The Picture of Dorian Gray

Young people, nowadays, imagine that money is everything ... and when they grow older they know it.

The Picture of Dorian Gray

You rich people in England, you don't know how you are living ... You shut out from your society the gentle and the good. You laugh at the simple and the pure ... With all your pomp and wealth and art you don't know how to live – you don't even know that.

A Woman of No Importance

Philanthropic people lose all sense of humanity. It is their distinguishing characteristic.

The Picture of Dorian Gray

… the way of paradoxes is the way of truth.

The Picture of Dorian Gray

Lying for the sake of gaining some immediate personal advantage, for instance – lying with a moral purpose, as it is usually called – though of late it has been rather looked down upon, was extremely popular with the antique world.

The Decay of Lying

I can sympathise with everything, except suffering.

The Picture of Dorian Gray

I like Wagner's music better than anybody's. It is so loud that one can talk the whole time without other people hearing what one says.

The Picture of Dorian Gray

Nowadays most people die of a sort of creeping common sense, and discover when it is too late that the only things one never regrets are one's mistakes.

The Picture of Dorian Gray

Many a man hath done so; sought to fence
In straitened bonds the soul that should be free,
Trodden the dusty road of common sense,
While all the forest sang of liberty, ...

"Apologia"

I am due at the Athenaeum. It is the hour when we sleep there … Forty of us in forty arm-chairs. We are practising for an English Academy of Letters.

The Picture of Dorian Gray

You seem quite out of sorts. You haven't quarrelled with your cook, I hope? What a tragedy that would be for you; you would lose all your friends.

Vera, or the Nihilists

… the people who love only once in their lives are really the shallow people. What they call their loyalty, and their fidelity, I call either the lethargy of custom or their lack of imagination. Faithfulness is to the emotional life what consistency is to the life of the intellect – simply a confession of failures.

The Picture of Dorian Gray

A great poet, a really great poet, is the most unpoetical of all creatures. But inferior poets are absolutely fascinating. The worse their rhymes are, the more picturesque they look.

The Picture of Dorian Gray

… no civilized man ever regrets a pleasure, and no uncivilized man ever knows what a pleasure is.

The Picture of Dorian Gray

There are only two kinds of people who are really fascinating – people who know absolutely everything, and people who know absolutely nothing.

The Picture of Dorian Gray

When we blame ourselves we feel that no one else has a right to blame us. It is the confession, not the priest, that gives us absolution.

The Picture of Dorian Gray

Good resolutions are useless attempts to interfere with scientific laws. Their origin is pure vanity. The result is absolutely nil. They give us, now and then, some of those luxurious sterile emotions that have a certain charm for the weak ... They are simply cheques that men draw on a bank where they have no account.

The Picture of Dorian Gray

Society, civilized society at least, is never very ready to believe anything to the detriment of those who are both rich and fascinating. It feels instinctively that manners are of more importance than morals ... it is a very poor consolation to be told that the man who has given one a bad dinner, or poor wine, is irreproachable in his private life.

The Picture of Dorian Gray

It is pure unadulterated country life. They get up early because they have so much to do, and go to bed early because they have so little to think about.

The Picture of Dorian Gray

Civilization is not by any means an easy thing to attain to. There are only two ways by which man can reach it. One is by being cultured, the other by being corrupt. Country people have no opportunity of being either, so they stagnate.

The Picture of Dorian Gray

The things one feels absolutely certain about are never true. That is the fatality of faith, and the lesson of Romance.

The Picture of Dorian Gray

To get back my youth I would do anything in the world, except take exercise, get up early, or be respectable.

The Picture of Dorian Gray

The books that the world calls immoral are books that show the world its own shame.

The Picture of Dorian Gray

I am always thinking about myself, and I expect everybody else to do the same. That is what is called sympathy.

The Remarkable Rocket

The only thing that sustains one through life is the consciousness of the immense inferiority of everybody else, and this is a feeling I have always cultivated.

The Remarkable Rocket

"Conversation, indeed … You have talked the whole time yourself. That is not conversation."

"Somebody must listen," answered the Frog, "and I like to do all the talking myself. It saves time, and prevents arguments."

The Remarkable Rocket

… there is nothing romantic about a definite proposal. Why, one may be accepted. One usually is, I believe. Then the excitement is all over. The very essence of romance is uncertainty.

The Importance of Being Earnest

Do you smoke? … I am glad to hear it. A man should always have an occupation of some kind.

The Importance of Being Earnest

I do not approve of anything that tampers with natural ignorance. Ignorance is like a delicate exotic fruit; touch it and the bloom is gone. The whole theory of modern education is radically unsound. Fortunately in England, at any rate, education produces no effect whatsoever. If it did, it would prove a serious danger to the upper classes, and probably lead to acts of violence in Grosvenor Square.

The Importance of Being Earnest

It is awfully hard work doing nothing. However, I don't mind hard work where there is no definite object of any kind.

The Importance of Being Earnest

If I am occasionally a little over-dressed, I make up for it by being always immensely over-educated.

The Importance of Being Earnest

It is always painful to part from people whom one has known for a very brief space of time. The absence of old friends one can endure with equanimity. But even a momentary separation from any one to whom one has just been introduced is almost unbearable.

The Importance of Being Earnest

Dr Chasuble is a most learned man. He has never written a single book, so you can imagine how much he knows.

The Importance of Being Earnest

Never speak disrespectfully of Society ... Only people who can't get into it do that.

The Importance of Being Earnest

… it is a terrible thing for a man to find out suddenly that all his life he has been speaking nothing but the truth.

The Importance of Being Earnest

Oh, nowadays so many conceited people go about Society pretending to be good, that I think it shows rather a sweet and modest disposition to pretend to be bad.

Lady Windermere's Fan

… good people do a great deal of harm in this world. Certainly the greatest harm they do is that they make badness of such extraordinary importance. It is absurd to divide people into good and bad. People are either charming or tedious.

Lady Windermere's Fan

… there are lots of people who say I have never really done anything wrong in the whole course of my life. Of course they only say it behind my back.

Lady Windermere's Fan

The youth of the present day are quite monstrous. They have absolutely no respect for dyed hair.

Lady Windermere's Fan.

… what a pity that in life we only get our lessons when they are of no use to us!

Lady Windermere's Fan

London is too full of fogs and – serious people … Whether the fogs produce the serious people or whether the serious people produce the fogs, I don't know …

Lady Windermere's Fan

Ideals are dangerous things. Realities are better. They wound, but they're better.

Lady Windermere's Fan

It is perfectly monstrous the way people go about, nowadays, saying things against one behind one's back that are absolutely and entirely true.

A Woman of No Importance

The intellect is not a serious thing and never has been. It is an instrument on which one plays, that is all. The only serious form of intellect I know is the British intellect. And on the British intellect the illiterates play the drum.

A Woman of No Importance

The soul is born old but grows young. That is the comedy of life ... And the body is born young and grows old. That is life's tragedy.

A Woman of No Importance

One can survive everything nowadays, except death, and live down anything except a good reputation.

A Woman of No Importance

I adore simple pleasures. They are the last refuge of the complex.

A Woman of No Importance

... after a good dinner one can forgive anybody, even one's own relations.

A Woman of No Importance

If a man is a gentleman, he knows quite enough, and if he is not a gentleman, whatever he knows is bad for him.

A Woman of No Importance

LORD ILLINGWORTH: To get into the best society, nowadays, one has either to feed people, amuse people, or shock people – that is all!

GERALD: I suppose society is wonderfully delightful!

LORD ILLINGWORTH: To be in it is merely a bore. But to be out of it simply a tragedy. Society is a necessary thing. No man has any real success in this world unless he has got women to back him, and women rule society. If you have not got women on your side you are quite over. You might just as well be a barrister or a stockbroker, or a journalist at once.

A Woman of No Importance

When one is in love one begins by deceiving oneself. And one ends by deceiving others. That is what the world calls a romance. But a really *grande passion* is comparatively rare nowadays. It is the privilege of people who have nothing to do. That is the one use of the idle classes in a country ...

A Woman of No Importance

You should study the Peerage ... It is the one book a young man about town should know thoroughly, and it is the best thing in fiction the English have ever done.

A Woman of No Importance

The only difference between the saint and the sinner is that every saint has a past, and every sinner has a future.

A Woman of No Importance

Savages seem to have quite the same views as cultured people on almost all subjects. They are excessively advanced.

A Woman of No Importance

∼⦙∼

Music makes one feel so romantic – at least it always gets on one's nerves.

A Woman of No Importance

∼⦙∼

I always pass on good advice. It is the only thing to do with it. It is never of any use to oneself.

An Ideal Husband

∼⦙∼

I tell you that there are terrible temptations that it requires strength, strength and courage, to yield to.

An Ideal Husband

Morality is simply the attitude we adopt towards people whom we personally dislike.

An Ideal Husband

LORD GORING: Extraordinary thing about the lower classes in England — they are always losing their relations.

PHIPPS: Yes, my lord! They are extremely fortunate in that respect.

An Ideal Husband

Really, I don't want to meet my father three days running. It is a great deal too much excitement for any son ... Fathers should be neither seen nor heard. That is the only proper basis for family life.

An Ideal Husband

… he has one of those terribly weak natures that are not susceptible to influence.

An Ideal Husband

What is the matter with this family? Something wrong here, eh? Idiocy? Hereditary, I suppose. Both of them, too. Wife as well as husband. Very sad. Very sad indeed! And they are not an old family. Can't understand it.

An Ideal Husband

Why, every man among them has his price,
Although to do them justice, some of them
Are quite expensive.

"The Duchess of Padua"

Ay! I can bear the ills of other men,
Which is philosophy.

"The Duchess of Padua"

In these modern days to be vulgar, illiterate, common and vicious, seems to give a man a marvellous infinity of rights that his honest fathers never dreamed of.

Vera, or the Nihilists

PRESIDENT [of the Nihilists]: ... The Nihilists never forget their friends, or forgive their enemies.
PRINCE PAUL: Really? I did not think you were so civilized.

Vera, or the Nihilists

Ah, the Grand Duke will come to the throne sooner that he expected. He is sure to make a good king under my guidance. He is so cruel to animals, and never keeps his word.

Vera, or the Nihilists

The first duty in life is to be as artificial as possible.
What the second duty is no one has as yet discovered.
   "Phrases and Philosophies for the Use of the Young"

Religions die when they are proved to be true. Science
is the record of dead religions.
   "Phrases and Philosophies for the Use of the Young"

Ambition is the last refuge of the failure.
   "Phrases and Philosophies for the Use of the Young"

A truth ceases to be true when more than one person
believes in it.
   "Phrases and Philosophies for the Use of the Young"

In examinations the foolish ask questions that the wise cannot answer.

"Phrases and Philosophies for the Use of the Young"

There is something tragic about the enormous number of young men there are in England at the present moment who start life with perfect profiles, and end by adopting some useful profession.

"Phrases and Philosophies for the Use of the Young"

Unless one is wealthy there is no use in being a charming fellow. Romance is the privilege of the rich, not the profession of the unemployed. The poor should be practical and prosaic. It is better to have a permanent income than to be fascinating.

The Model Millionaire

Religion consoles some. Its mysteries have all the charm of a flirtation, a woman once told me, and I can understand it. Besides nothing makes one so vain as being told that one is a sinner.

The Picture of Dorian Gray

A man cannot always be estimated by what he does. He may keep the law, and yet be worthless. He may break the law, and yet be fine. He may be bad, without ever doing anything bad.

The Soul of Man under Socialism

There is not a single real poet or prose-writer of this century ... on whom the British public have not solemnly conferred diplomas of immorality, and these diplomas practically take the place, with us, of what in France is the formal recognition of an Academy of Letters, and fortunately makes the establishment of such an institution quite unnecessary in England.

The Soul of Man under Socialism

... it is only fair to state, with regard to modern journalists, that they always apologize to one in private for what they have written against one in public.

The Soul of Man under Socialism

~ ·•· ~

In the old days men had the rack. Now they have the Press.

The Soul of Man under Socialism

~ ·•· ~

English public opinion ... tries to constrain and impede and warp the man who makes things that are beautiful in effect, and compels the journalist to retail things that are ugly, or disgusting, or revolting in fact, so that we have the most serious journalists in the world and the most indecent newspapers.

The Soul of Man under Socialism

The bad Popes loved Beauty ... with as much passion as the good Popes hated Thought.

The Soul of Man under Socialism

The ancient historians gave us delightful fiction in the form of fact; the modern novelist presents us with dull facts under the guise of fiction.

The Decay of Lying

The crude commercialism of America, its materializing spirit, its indifference to the poetical side of things, and its lack of imagination and of high unattainable ideals, are entirely due to that country having adopted for its national hero a man who, according to his own confession, was incapable of telling a lie.

The Decay of Lying

A short primer, "When to Lie and How", if brought out in an attractive and not too expensive a form, would no doubt command a large sale, and would prove of real practical service to many earnest and deep-thinking people.

The Decay of Lying

At twilight nature becomes a wonderfully suggestive effect, and is not without loveliness, though perhaps its chief use is to illustrate quotations from the poets.

The Decay of Lying

My father would talk morality after dinner. I told him he was old enough to know better. But my experience is that as soon as people are old enough to know better, they don't know anything at all.

Lady Windermere's Fan

I should fancy, however, that murder is always a mistake. One should never do anything that one cannot talk about after dinner.

The Picture of Dorian Gray

Lying for the sake of the improvement of the young, which is the basis of home education, still lingers amongst us.

The Decay of Lying

Hopper is one of Nature's gentlemen, the worst type of gentleman I know.

Lady Windermere's Fan

My own business always bores me to death. I prefer other people's.

Lady Windermere's Fan

Oh! gossip is charming! History is merely gossip. But scandal is gossip made tedious by moralizing.

Lady Windermere's Fan

Experience is the name everyone gives to their mistakes. That is all.

Lady Windermere's Fan

One has never heard his name before in the whole course of one's life, which speaks volumes for a man, nowadays.

A Woman of No Importance

… what consoles one nowadays is not repentance, but pleasure. Repentance is quite out of date.

Lady Windermere's Fan

HESTER: We have the largest country in the world, Lady Caroline. They used to tell us at school that some of our states are as big as France and England put together.

LADY CAROLINE: Ah! You must find it very draughty, I should fancy.

A Woman of No Importance

Oh! Life is terrible. It rules us, we do not rule it.

Lady Windermere's Fan

Actions are the first tragedy in life, words are the second.

Lady Windermere's Fan

She certainly has a wonderful faculty of remembering people's names and forgetting their faces.

A Woman of No Importance

But somehow, I feel sure that if I lived in the country for six months, I should become so unsophisticated that no one would take the slightest notice of me.

A Woman of No Importance

I think to elope is cowardly. It's running away from danger. And danger has become so rare in modern life.

A Woman of No Importance

The one advantage of playing with fire ... is that one never gets even singed. It is the people who don't know how to play with it who get burned up.

A Woman of No Importance

KELVIL: I find that the poorer classes of the country display a marked desire for a higher ethical standard.
LADY STUTFIELD: How quite, quite nice of them.

A Woman of No Importance

MRS ALLONBY: They say, Lady Hunstanton, that when good Americans die they go to Paris.

LADY HUNSTANTON: Indeed? And when bad Americans die, where do they go to?

LORD ILLINGWORTH: Oh, they go to America.

A Woman of No Importance

~ ❧ ~

One should never take sides in anything … Taking sides is the beginning of sincerity, and earnestness follows shortly afterwards, and the human being becomes a bore.

A Woman of No Importance

~ ❧ ~

KELVIL: May I ask, Lord Illingworth, if you regard the House of Lords as a better institution than the House of Commons?

LORD ILLINGWORTH: A much better institution, of course. We in the House of Lords are never in touch with public opinion. That makes us a civilized body.

A Woman of No Importance

LADY STUTFIELD: Do you really, really think, Lady Caroline, that one should believe evil of everyone?

LADY CAROLINE: I think it is much safer to do so, Lady Stutfield. Until, of course, people are found out to be good. But that requires a great deal of investigation nowadays.

A Woman of No Importance

LADY STUTFIELD: But don't the people to whom you owe the money give you a great, great deal of annoyance?

LORD ALFRED: Oh, no, they write; I don't.

A Woman of No Importance

HESTER: I dislike London dinner-parties.

MRS ALLONBY: I adore them. The clever people never listen, and the stupid people never talk.

HESTER: I think the stupid people talk a great deal.

MRS ALLONBY: Ah, I never listen.

A Woman of No Importance

MRS ALLONBY: Have you tried a good reputation?
LORD ILLINGWORTH: It is one of the many annoyances
to which I have never been subjected.

A Woman of No Importance

~❧~

HESTER: In America we have no lower classes.
LADY HUNSTANTON: Really? What a very strange
arrangement!

A Woman of No Importance

~❧~

[Of USA] The English aristocracy supply us with our
curiosities ... They are sent over to us every summer,
regularly in the steamers, and propose to us the day
after they land. As for ruins, we are trying to build up
something that will last longer than brick or stone.

A Woman of No Importance

All Americans lecture, I believe. I suppose it is something in their climate.

A Woman of No Importance

A man who can dominate a London dinner-table can
dominate the world. The future belongs to the dandy.
It is the exquisites who are going to rule.

A Woman of No Importance

People nowadays are so absolutely superficial that they
don't understand the philosophy of the superficial.

A Woman of No Importance

For the world has been made by fools that wise men
should live in it.

A Woman of No Importance

... the world has always laughed at its own tragedies, that being the only way in which it has been able to bear them. And that, consequently, whatever the world has treated seriously belongs to the comedy side of things.

A Woman of No Importance

The world is simply divided into two classes – those who believe the incredible, like the public – and those who do the improbable ...

A Woman of No Importance

MRS ALLONBY: The secret of life is never to have an emotion that is unbecoming.

LADY STUTFIELD: The secret of life is to appreciate the pleasure of being terribly, terribly deceived.

KELVIL: The secret of life is to resist temptation, Lady Stutfield.

LORD ILLINGWORTH: There is no secret of life. Life's aim, if it has one, is simply to be always looking for temptations. There are not nearly enough. I sometimes pass a whole day without coming across a single one. It is quite dreadful. It makes one so nervous about the future.

A Woman of No Importance

All thought is immoral. Its very essence is destruction. If you think of anything, you kill it. Nothing survives being thought of.

A Woman of No Importance

LORD ILLINGWORTH: As for a title, a title is really rather a nuisance in these democratic days. As George Harford I had everything I wanted. Now I have merely everything that other people want, which isn't nearly so pleasant.

A Woman of No Importance

Why, he rides in the Row at ten o'clock in the morning, goes to the Opera three times a week, changes his clothes at least five times a day, and dines out every night of the season. You don't call that leading an idle life, do you?

An Ideal Husband

Oh! I love London Society! I think it has immensely improved. It is entirely composed now of beautiful idiots and brilliant lunatics. Just what Society should be.

An Ideal Husband

It would be inaccurate to call him picturesque. Picturesqueness cannot survive the House of Commons.

An Ideal Husband

Really, now that the House of Commons is trying to become useful, it does a great deal of harm.

An Ideal Husband

Families are so mixed nowadays. Indeed, as a rule, everybody turns out to be somebody else.

An Ideal Husband

An acquaintance that begins with a compliment is sure to develop into a real friendship. It starts in the right manner.

An Ideal Husband

SIR ROBERT CHILTERN: ... are you an optimist or a pessimist? Those seem to be the only two fashionable religions left to us nowadays.

MRS CHEVELY: Oh, I'm neither. Optimism begins in a broad grin, and Pessimism ends with blue spectacles. Besides, they are both of them merely poses.

An Ideal Husband

Questions are never indiscreet. Answers sometimes are.

An Ideal Husband

And philanthropy seems to me to have become simply the refuge of people who wish to annoy their fellow-creatures.

An Ideal Husband

Oh! I am not at all romantic. I am not old enough. I leave romance to my seniors.

An Ideal Husband

❧

MABEL CHILTERN: You are always telling me of your bad qualities, Lord Goring.
LORD GORING: I have only told you half of them as yet, Miss Mabel!
MABEL CHILTERN: Are the others very bad?
LORD GORING: Quite dreadful! When I think of them at night I go to sleep at once.

An Ideal Husband

❧

MABEL CHILTERN: ... Aren't you coming to the music-room?
LORD GORING: Not if there is any music going on, Miss Mabel.
MABEL CHILTERN: The music is in German. You would not understand it.

An Ideal Husband

LORD GORING: I love talking about nothing, father. It is the only thing I know anything about.

LORD CAVERSHAM: You seem to me to be living entirely for pleasure.

LORD GORING: What else is there to live for, father? Nothing ages like happiness.

An Ideal Husband

LORD GORING: I adore political parties. They are the only place left to us where people don't talk politics.

LADY BASILDON: I delight in talking politics. I talk them all day long. But I can't bear listening to them. I don't know how the unfortunate men in the House stand these long debates.

LORD GORING: By never listening.

An Ideal Husband

I like looking at geniuses, and listening to beautiful people.

An Ideal Husband

I am so fond of eating! I am very English in all my tastes.

An Ideal Husband

~ ❧ ~

I can't stand your English house-parties. In England people actually try to be brilliant at breakfast. That is so dreadful of them! Only dull people are brilliant at breakfast.

An Ideal Husband

~ ❧ ~

In modern life nothing produces such an effect as a good platitude.

An Ideal Husband

~ ❧ ~

One should always play fairly ... when one has the winning cards.

An Ideal Husband

I am a little too old now, myself, to trouble about setting a good example, but I always admire people who do.

An Ideal Husband

... I am thoroughly sick of pearls. They make one look so plain, so good, and so intellectual.

An Ideal Husband

I had the double misfortune of being well-born and poor, two unforgivable things nowadays.

An Ideal Husband

SIR ROBERT CHILTERN: ... he was a man of a most subtle and refined intellect. A man of culture, charm, and distinction. One of the most intellectual men I ever met.

LORD GORING: Ah! I prefer a gentlemanly fool any day. There is more to be said for stupidity than people imagine ...

An Ideal Husband

... when the gods wish to punish us they answer our prayers.

An Ideal Husband

I am always saying what I shouldn't say. In fact, I usually say what I really think. A great mistake nowadays. It makes one so liable to be misunderstood.

An Ideal Husband

... the English can't stand a man who is always saying he is in the right, but they are very fond of a man who admits that he has been in the wrong.

An Ideal Husband

It is always worthwhile asking a question, though it is not always worthwhile answering one.

An Ideal Husband

... the truth is a thing a get rid of as soon as possible!

An Ideal Husband

Nothing is so dangerous as being too modern. One is apt to grow old-fashioned quite suddenly.

An Ideal Husband

Other people are quite dreadful. The only possible society is oneself.

An Ideal Husband

However, it is always nice to be expected, and not to arrive.

An Ideal Husband

Oh, damn sympathy. There is a great deal too much of that sort of thing going on nowadays.

An Ideal Husband

If there was less sympathy in the world there would be less trouble in the world.

An Ideal Husband

Everybody one meets is a paradox nowadays. It is a great bore. It makes society so obvious.

An Ideal Husband

To expect the unexpected shows a thoroughly modern intellect.

An Ideal Husband

Oh! spies are of no use nowadays. Their profession is over. The newspapers do their work instead.

An Ideal Husband

I have a perfect passion for listening through keyholes. One always hears such wonderful things through them.

An Ideal Husband

I don't think anyone at all morally responsible for
what he or she does at an English country house.

An Ideal Husband

... self-sacrifice is a thing that should be put down by
law. It is so demoralizing to the people for whom one
sacrifices oneself. They always go to the bad.

An Ideal Husband

... when one pays a visit it is for the purpose of
wasting other people's time, not one's own.

An Ideal Husband

... only people who look dull ever get into the House
of Commons, and only people who are dull ever
succeed there.

An Ideal Husband

You love the beauty that you can see and touch and handle, the beauty that you can destroy, and do destroy . . . but of the unseen beauty of a higher life, you know nothing. You have lost life's secret.

A Woman of No Importance

I don't at all like knowing what people say of me behind my back. It makes me far too conceited.

An Ideal Husband

I don't like principles . . . I prefer prejudices.

An Ideal Husband

As far as the piano is concerned, sentiment is my forte. I keep science for Life.

The Importance of Being Earnest

Really, if the lower orders don't set us a good example, what on earth is the use of them? They seem, as a class, to have absolutely no sense of moral responsibility.

The Importance of Being Earnest

… I don't propose to discuss modern culture. It isn't the sort of thing one should talk of in private.

The Importance of Being Earnest

It is very vulgar to talk like a dentist when one isn't a dentist. It produces a false impression.

The Importance of Being Earnest

If you pretend to be good, the world takes you seriously. If you pretend to be bad, it doesn't. Such is the astounding stupidity of optimism.

Lady Windermere's Fan

... I am afraid that good people do a great deal of harm in this world. Certainly the greatest harm they do is that they make badness of such extraordinary importance.

Lady Windermere's Fan

As a wicked man I am a complete failure. Why, there are lots of people who say I have never really done anything wrong in the whole course of my life. Of course they only say it behind my back.

Lady Windermere's Fan

Nowadays to be intelligible is to be found out.

Lady Windermere's Fan

Demmed nuisance, relations! But they make one so demmed respectable.

Lady Windermere's Fan

When one is placed in the position of guardian, one has to adopt a very high moral tone on all subjects. It's one's duty to do so. And as a high moral tone can hardly be said to conduce very much to either one's health or one's happiness, in order to get up to town I have always pretended to have a younger brother of the name of Ernest ...

The Importance of Being Earnest

Literary criticism is not your forte, my dear fellow. Don't try it. You should leave that to people who haven't been at a University. They do it so well in the daily papers.

The Importance of Being Earnest

Nothing annoys people so much as not receiving invitations.

The Importance of Being Earnest

JACK: You're quite perfect, Miss Fairfax.

GWENDOLEN: Oh! I hope I am not that. It would leave no room for developments, and I intend to develop in many directions.

The Importance of Being Earnest

I hadn't been there since her poor husband's death. I never saw a woman so altered; she looks quite twenty years younger.

The Importance of Being Earnest

I hear her hair has turned quite gold from grief.

The Importance of Being Earnest

Nor do I in any way approve of the modern sympathy with invalids. I consider it morbid. Illness of any kind is hardly a thing to be encouraged in others.

The Importance of Being Earnest

… if one plays good music, people don't listen, and if one plays bad music people don't talk.

The Importance of Being Earnest

French songs I cannot possibly allow. People always seem to think that they are improper, and either look shocked, which is vulgar, or laugh, which is worse. But German sounds a thoroughly respectable language, and, indeed, I believe it is so.

The Importance of Being Earnest

Pray don't talk to me about the weather … Whenever people talk to me about the weather, I always feel quite certain that they mean something else. And that makes me nervous.

The Importance of Being Earnest

JACK: … I don't much care about the name of Ernest … I don't think the name suits me at all.

GWENDOLEN: It suits you perfectly. It is a divine name. It has music of its own. It produces vibrations.

The Importance of Being Earnest

I have known several Jacks, and they all, without exception, were more than usually plain. Besides, Jack is a notorious domesticity for John! And I pity any woman who is married to a man called John. She would probably never be allowed to know the entrancing pleasure of a single moment's solitude.

The Importance of Being Earnest

JACK: … She is a lady considerably advanced in years.

LADY BRACKNELL: Ah, nowadays that is no guarantee of respectability of character.

The Importance of Being Earnest

A girl with a simple, unspoiled nature, like Gwendolen, could hardly be expected to reside in the country.

The Importance of Being Earnest

To lose one parent ... may be regarded as a misfortune; to lose both looks like carelessness.

The Importance of Being Earnest

The simplicity of your character makes you exquisitely incomprehensible to me.

The Importance of Being Earnest

My dear boy, I love hearing my relations abused. It is the only thing that makes me put up with them at all.

The Importance of Being Earnest

I am sick to death of cleverness. Everybody is clever nowadays. You can't go anywhere without meeting clever people. The thing has become an absolute public nuisance. I wish to goodness we had a few fools left.

The Importance of Being Earnest

Few parents nowadays pay any regard to what their children say to them. The old-fashioned respect for the young is fast dying out. Whatever influence I ever had over mamma, I lost at the age of three.

The Importance of Being Earnest

To be born, or at any rate bred, in a hand-bag, whether it had handles or not, seems to me to display a contempt for the ordinary decencies of family life that reminds me of the excesses of the French Revolution.

The Importance of Being Earnest

ALGERNON: I hope tomorrow will be a fine day, Lane.

LANE: It never is, sir.

ALGERNON: Lane, you're a perfect pessimist.

LANE: I do my best to give satisfaction, sir.

The Importance of Being Earnest

I am not in favour of this modern mania for turning bad people into good people at a moment's notice.

The Importance of Being Earnest

I keep a diary in order to enter the wonderful secrets of my life. If I didn't write them down, I should probably forget all about them.

The Importance of Being Earnest

I have never met any really wicked person before. I feel rather frightened. I am so afraid he will look just like every one else.

The Importance of Being Earnest

I hope you have not been leading a double life, pretending to be wicked and being really good all the time. That would be hypocrisy.

The Importance of Being Earnest

Well, I know, of course, how important it is not to keep a business engagement, if one wants to retain any sense of the beauty of life …

The Importance of Being Earnest

I don't think you will require neckties. Uncle Jack is sending you to Australia.

The Importance of Being Earnest

The accounts I have received of Australia and the next world are not particularly encouraging.

The Importance of Being Earnest

None of us are perfect. I myself am peculiarly susceptible to draughts.

The Importance of Being Earnest

My duty as a gentleman has never interfered with my
pleasures in the smallest degree.

The Importance of Being Earnest

I never saw anybody take so long to dress, and with
such little result.

The Importance of Being Earnest

ALGERNON: Do you really keep a diary? I'd give
anything to look at it. May I?
CECILY: Oh no. You see, it is simply a very young girl's
record of her own thoughts and impressions, and
consequently meant for publication. When it appears
in volume form I hope you will order a copy.

The Importance of Being Earnest

Yes, you've wonderfully good taste … It's the excuse
I've always given for your leading such a bad life.

The Importance of Being Earnest

GWENDOLEN: … Cecily, mamma, whose views on
education are remarkably strict, has brought me up to
be extremely short-sighted; it is part of her system; so
do you mind my looking at you through my glasses?
CECILY: Oh! not at all, Gwendolen. I am very fond of
being looked at.

The Importance of Being Earnest

I am glad to say that I have never seen a spade. It is
obvious that our social spheres have been widely
different.

The Importance of Being Earnest

What on earth you are serious about I haven't got the remotest idea. About everything, I should fancy. You have such an absolutely trivial nature.

The Importance of Being Earnest

Indeed, when I am in really great trouble … I refuse everything except food and drink.

The Importance of Being Earnest

I never go without my dinner. It's absurd. No one ever does, except vegetarians and people like that.

The Importance of Being Earnest

They have been eating muffins. That looks like repentance.

The Importance of Being Earnest

Hesitation of any kind is a sign of mental decay in the young, of physical weakness in the old.

The Importance of Being Earnest

Three addresses always inspire confidence, even in tradesmen.

The Importance of Being Earnest

There are distinct social possibilities in your profile. The two weak points in our age are its want of principle and its want of profile.

The Importance of Being Earnest

I am not punctual myself, I know, but I do like punctuality in others, and waiting, even to be married, is quite out of the question.

The Importance of Being Earnest

LADY BRACKNELL: ... Is this Miss Prism a female of repellent aspect, remotely connected with education?

CHASUBLE: She is the most cultivated of ladies, and the very picture of respectability.

LADY BRACKNELL: It is obviously the same person.

The Importance of Being Earnest

He was eccentric, I admit. But only in later years. And that was the result of the Indian climate, and marriage, and indigestion, and other things of the kind.

The Importance of Being Earnest

JACK: Gwendolen, it is a terrible thing for a man to find out suddenly that all his life he has been speaking nothing but the truth. Can you forgive me?

GWENDOLEN: I can. For I feel that you are sure to change.

The Importance of Being Earnest

I think half-an-hour's warping of the inner man is greatly conducive to holiness.

The Importance of Being Earnest

I am sure you will be interested to hear that I have met [American] Indians. They are really in appearance very like Colvin [a Cambridge art professor], when he is wearing his professorial robes: the likeness is quite curious, and revived pleasant literary reminiscences. Their conversation was most interesting as long as it was unintelligible.

Letters

Jesse James had just been killed by one of his followers, and the whole town was mourning over him and buying relics of his house. His door-knocker and dust-bin went for fabulous prices, two speculators absolutely came to pistol-shots as to who was to have his hearth-brush, the unsuccessful one being, however, consoled by being allowed to purchase the water-butt for the income of an English bishop, while his sole work of art, a chromo-lithograph of the most dreadful kind, of course was sold at a price which in Europe only a Mantegna or an undoubted Titian can command!

Letters

They drove me out to see the great prison afterwards! Poor odd types of humanity in hideous striped dresses making bricks in the sun, and all mean-looking, which consoled me, for I should hate to see a criminal with a noble face.

Letters

[Of his fiancée] ... however, she knows I am the greatest poet, so in literature she is all right: and I have explained to her that you are the greatest sculptor: art instruction cannot go further.

Letters

The baby is wonderful: it has a bridge to its nose! which the nurse says is a proof of genius! It also has a superb voice, which it freely exercises: its style is essentially Wagnerian.

Letters

It is a sad thing, but one wearies even of praise.

Letters

One has merely to read the ordinary English newspapers and the ordinary English novels of our day to become conscious of the fact that it is only the obvious that occurs, and only the obvious that is written about.

Letters

In London we have merely the ill-clad newsvendors, whose voice, in spite of the admirable efforts of the Royal College of Music to make England a really musical nation, is always out of tune, and whose rags, badly designed and badly worn, merely emphasize a painful note of uncomely misery, without conveying that impression of picturesqueness which is the only thing that makes the spectacle of the poverty of others at all bearable.

Letters

Tree has written a long apologetic letter. His reasons are so reasonable that I cannot understand them: a cheque is the only argument I recognize.

Letters

London is very dangerous: writters come out at night and writ one, the roaring of creditors towards dawn is frightful, and solicitors are getting rabies and biting people.

Letters

～•～

There was no harm in your seriously considering that the most perfect way of passing an evening was to have a champagne dinner at the Savoy, a box at a Music-Hall to follow, and a champagne supper at Willis's as a bonne-bouche for the end. Heaps of delightful young men in London are of the same opinion. It is not even an eccentricity. It is the qualification for becoming a member of White's.

Letters

～•～

The fact that your father loathed you, and that you loathed your father, was not a matter of any interest to the English public. Such feelings are very common in English domestic life, and should be confined to the place they characterize: the home.

Letters

... the type-writing machine, when played with expression, is not more annoying than the piano when played by a sister or near relation. Indeed many, among those most devoted to domesticity, prefer it.

Letters

I hate mystery. It is so obvious.

Letters

I am going to write a Political Economy in my heavier moments. The first law I lay down is "Wherever there exists a demand, there is no supply." This is the only law that explains the extraordinary contrast between the soul of man, and man's surroundings. Civilizations continue because people hate them. A modern city is the exact opposite of what everyone wants. Nineteenth-century dress is the result of our horror of the style. The tall hat will last as long as people dislike it.

Letters

Once you get to fight duels in France, you have to be always doing it, and it is a nuisance.

Letters

[Of duels] And though it is not dangerous, like our English cricket or football is, still it is a tedious game to be always playing.

Letters

There is no difference between gentlemen. Questions of titles are matters of heraldry – no more.

Letters

He founded a school, and has survived all his disciples. He has always thought too much about himself, which is wise; and written too much about others, which is foolish. His prose is the beautiful prose of a poet, and his poetry the beautiful poetry of a prose-writer.

Letters

But in questions of the emotions and their romantic qualities, unpunctuality is fatal.

Letters

By "Caiaphas" I do not mean the present Chaplain of Reading: he is a good-natured fool, one of the silliest of God's silly sheep: a typical clergyman in fact.

Letters

And Financial Problems can by solved only by Finance. Genius, Art, Romance, Passion, and the like are useless when the point at issue is one of figures. A solution for an algebraic problem is not to be found in the sense of Beauty, however developed.

Letters

The popularity of the poem will be largely increased by the author's painful death by starvation. The public love poets to die in that way. It seems to them dramatically right. Perhaps it is.

Letters

Bosie [Lord Alfred Douglas] is of course a gilded pillar of infamy in this century, but whether he is legally disreputable is another question.

Letters

I suppose publishers are untrustworthy. They certainly always look it.

Letters

I am very glad you went to Margate, which, I believe is the nom-de-plume of Ramsgate. It is a quiet nice spot not vulgarized by crowds of literary people.

Letters

People don't understand that criticism is prejudice, because to understand one must love, and to love one must have passion. It is only the unimaginative who are ever fair.

Letters

The present prison system seems almost to have for its aim the wrecking and the destruction of the mental faculties. The production of insanity is, if not its object, certainly its result.

Letters

People who repent in sackcloth are dreary, but those who repent in a suit by Dore, and intend this suit for another, are worthy of Paradise.

Letters

It is an entirely English trait, the English type and symbol of a joke being the jug on the half-opened door, or the distribution of orange-peel on the pavement of a crowded thoroughfare.

Letters

～🔔～

To undress is romance, to dress, philanthropy.

Letters

～🔔～

Dogma without literature is bad for boys.

Letters

～🔔～

I am going to try a bicycle. I have never forgotten the lesson you so kindly gave me: even my leg remembers it.

Letters

Like dear St Francis of Assisi I am wedded to Poverty:
but in my case the marriage is not a success.

Letters

… and looking at angels, or indeed at people singing,
is much nicer than listening to them. For this reason
the great artists always give to their angels lutes
without strings, pipes without vent-holes, and reeds
through which no wind can wander or make
whistlings.

Letters

Cows are very fond of being photographed, and,
unlike architecture, don't move.

Letters

[In Rome] The pilgrims arrive in great black swarms: I am sure that Pharaoh was punished by a plague of them: some of them, however, go mad. Three cases yesterday. They are much envied by their more sane brethren.

Letters

… the automobile was delightful, but, of course, it broke down: they, like all machines, are more wilful than animals – nervous, irritable, strange things: I am going to write an article on "nerves in the inorganic world."

Letters

At present he has almost arrived at total abstinence – drinks and talks mineral waters. I like people who talk wine.

Letters

A bishop keeps on saying at the age of eighty what he was told to say when he was a boy of eighteen, and as a natural consequence he always looks absolutely delightful.

The Picture of Dorian Gray

… and as for believing things, I can believe anything, provided that it is quite incredible.

The Picture of Dorian Gray

With an evening coat and a white tie, as you told me once, anybody, even a stockbroker, can gain a reputation for being civilized.

The Picture of Dorian Gray

I believe some picture of mine had made a great success at the time, at least had been chattered about in the penny newspapers, which is the nineteenth-century standard of immortality.

The Picture of Dorian Gray

But Lady Brandon treats her guests exactly as an
auctioneer treats his goods. She either explains them
entirely away, or tells one everything about them
except what one wants to know.

The Picture of Dorian Gray

But I can't help detesting my relations. I suppose it
comes from the fact that none of us can stand other
people having the same faults as ourselves.

The Picture of Dorian Gray

I like persons better than principles, and I like persons
with no principles better than anything else in the
world.

The Picture of Dorian Gray

… the worst of having a romance of any kind is that it
leaves one so unromantic.

The Picture of Dorian Gray

The rich would have spoken on the value of thrift, and the idle grown eloquent over the dignity of labour.

The Picture of Dorian Gray

The mutilation of the savage has its tragic survival in the self-denial that mars our lives. We are punished for our refusals. Every impulse that we strive to strangle broods in the mind, and poisons us.

The Picture of Dorian Gray

The only way to get rid of a temptation is to yield to it. Resist it, and your soul grows sick with longing for the things it has forbidden to itself, with desire for what its monstrous laws have made monstrous and unlawful.

The Picture of Dorian Gray

It is in the brain, and the brain only, that the great sins of the world take place also.

The Picture of Dorian Gray

He has certainly not been paying me compliments. Perhaps that is the reason that I don't believe anything he has told me.

The Picture of Dorian Gray

People say sometimes that Beauty is only superficial. That may be so. But at least it is not so superficial as Thought is.

The Picture of Dorian Gray

"I can't bear the idea of my soul being hideous."
"A very charming artistic basis for ethics, Dorian!"

The Picture of Dorian Gray

What a fuss people make about fidelity! ... Why, even in love it is purely a question for physiology. It has nothing to do with our own will.

The Picture of Dorian Gray

His father had been our ambassador at Madrid ... but had retired from the Diplomatic Service in a capricious moment of annoyance at not being offered the Embassy at Paris, a post to which he considered that he was fully entitled by reason of his birth, his indolence, the good English of his despatches, and his inordinate passion for pleasure.

The Picture of Dorian Gray

The advantage of the emotions is that they lead us astray, and the advantage of Science is that it is not emotional.

The Picture of Dorian Gray

Next to her sat ... Sir Thomas Burdon, a Radical member of Parliament, who followed his leader in public life, and in private life followed the best cooks, dining with the Tories, and thinking with the Liberals, in accordance with a wise and well-known rule.

The Picture of Dorian Gray

Perhaps, after all, America never has been discovered ... I myself would say it had merely been detected.

The Picture of Dorian Gray

I know, now, that when one loses one's good looks, whatever they may be, one loses everything.

The Picture of Dorian Gray

To get back one's youth, one has merely to repeat one's follies.

The Picture of Dorian Gray

You have never been to any of my parties, have you, Mr Gray? You must come. I can't afford orchids, but I spare no expense in foreigners. They make one's rooms look so picturesque.

The Picture of Dorian Gray

She was usually in love with somebody, and, as her passion was never returned she had kept all her illusions.

The Picture of Dorian Gray

I have simply worshipped pianists — two at a time, sometimes … I don't know what it is about them. Perhaps it is that they are foreigners. They all are, ain't they? Even those that are born in England become foreigners after a time, don't they? It is so clever of them, as such a compliment to art.

The Picture of Dorian Gray

He was always late on principle, his principle being that punctuality is the thief of time.

The Picture of Dorian Gray

Faithfulness! I must analyse it some day. The passion for property is in it. There are many things that we would throw away if we were not afraid that others might pick them up.

The Picture of Dorian Gray

"... Harry! why didn't you tell me that the only thing worth loving is an actress?"
"Because I have loved so many of them, Dorian."
"Oh, yes, horrid people with dyed hair and painted faces."
"Don't run down dyed hair and painted faces. There is an extraordinary charm in them sometimes."

The Picture of Dorian Gray

It is only the sacred things that are worth touching …
The Picture of Dorian Gray

~§~

There is always something infinitely mean about other people's tragedies.
The Picture of Dorian Gray

~§~

One could never pay too high a price for any sensation.
The Picture of Dorian Gray

~§~

But there was no motive power in experience. It was as little an active cause as conscience itself. All that it really demonstrated was that our future would be the same as our past, and that the sin we had done once, and with loathing, we would do many times, and with joy.

The Picture of Dorian Gray

There is hardly a single person in the House of Commons worth painting; though many of them would be the better for a little white-washing.

The Picture of Dorian Gray

"Dorian is far too wise not to do foolish things now and then, my dear Basil."

"Marriage is hardly a thing that one can do now and then, Harry."

"Except in America," rejoined Lord Henry, languidly.

The Picture of Dorian Gray

Whenever a man does a thoroughly stupid thing, it is always from the noblest motives.

The Picture of Dorian Gray

I never approve, or disapprove, of anything now. It is an absurd attitude to take towards life. We are not sent into the world to air our moral prejudices. I never take any notice of what common people say, and I never interfere with what charming people do.

The Picture of Dorian Gray

Yes, we are overcharged for everything nowadays. I should fancy that the real tragedy of the poor is that they can afford nothing but self-denial. Beautiful sins, like beautiful things, are the privilege of the rich.

The Picture of Dorian Gray

I asked the question for the best reason possible, for the only reason, indeed, that excuses one for asking any question – simply curiosity.

The Picture of Dorian Gray

To be good is to be in harmony with one's self ...
Discord is to be forced to be in harmony with others.

The Picture of Dorian Gray

As for a spoiled life, no life is spoiled but one whose growth is arrested. If you want to mar a nature, you have merely to reform it.

The Picture of Dorian Gray

A cigarette is the perfect type of a perfect pleasure. It is exquisite, and it leaves one unsatisfied. What more can one want?

The Picture of Dorian Gray

There was a rather heavy bill … that he had not had the courage to send on to his guardians, who were extremely old-fashioned people and did not realize that we live in an age when unnecessary things are our only necessities …

The Picture of Dorian Gray

Here one should never make one's debut with a scandal. One should reserve that to give an interest to one's old age.

The Picture of Dorian Gray

We live in an age that reads too much to be wise, and that thinks too much to be beautiful.

The Picture of Dorian Gray

I cannot repeat an emotion. No one can, except senti-mentalists.

The Picture of Dorian Gray

You came down here to console me. That is charming of you. You find me consoled and you are furious. How like a sympathetic person!

The Picture of Dorian Gray

… and certainly the Roman [Catholic] ritual had always a great attraction for him. The daily sacrifice, more awful really than all the sacrifices of the antique world, stirred him as much by its superb rejection of the evidence of the senses as by the primitive simplicity of its elements and the eternal pathos of the human tragedy that it sought to symbolize.

The Picture of Dorian Gray

I love scandals about other people, but scandals about myself don't interest me. They have not got the charm of novelty.

The Picture of Dorian Gray

The middle classes air their moral prejudices over their gross dinner-tables, and whisper about what they call the profligacies of their betters in order to try and pretend that they are in smart society, and on intimate terms with the people they slander.

The Picture of Dorian Gray

There were sins whose fascination was more in the memory than in the doing of them; strange triumphs that gratified the pride more than the passions, and gave to the intellect a quickened sense of joy, greater than any joy they brought, or could ever bring, to the senses.

The Picture of Dorian Gray

… one of those middle-aged mediocrities so common in London clubs who have no enemies, but are thoroughly disliked by their friends.

The Picture of Dorian Gray

… Lady Alice Chapman, his hostess's daughter, a dowdy dull girl, with one of those characteristic British faces, that, once seen, are never remembered.

The Picture of Dorian Gray

Her capacity for family affection is extraordinary. When her third husband dies, her hair turned quite gold from grief.

The Picture of Dorian Gray

… don't tell me that you have exhausted Life. When a man says that one knows that Life has exhausted him.

The Picture of Dorian Gray

Moderation is a fatal thing. Enough is as bad as a meal. More than enough is as good as a feast.

The Picture of Dorian Gray

The inherited stupidity of the race – sound English common sense he jovially termed it – was shown to be the proper bulwark for Society.

The Picture of Dorian Gray

~•~

I admit that I think that it is better to be beautiful than to be good. But on the other hand no one is more ready than I am to acknowledge that it is better to be good than to be ugly.

The Picture of Dorian Gray

~•~

Ugliness is one of the seven deadly virtues … Beer, the Bible, and the seven deadly virtues have made our England what she is.

The Picture of Dorian Gray

~•~

Every effect that one produces gives one an enemy. To be popular one must be a mediocrity.

The Picture of Dorian Gray

Romance lives by repetition, and repetition converts as appetite into an art. Besides, each time that one loves is the only time one has ever loved. Difference of object does not alter singleness of passion. It merely intensifies it.

The Picture of Dorian Gray

I have never searched for happiness. Who wants happiness? I have searched for pleasure.

The Picture of Dorian Gray

The only horrible thing in the world is ennui ... That is the one sin for which there is no forgiveness.

The Picture of Dorian Gray

... anybody can be good in the country. There are no temptations there.

The Picture of Dorian Gray

My dear boy, they have only been talking about it for six weeks, and the British public are really not equal to the mental strain of having more than one topic every three months.

The Picture of Dorian Gray

Death and vulgarity are the only two facts in the nineteenth century that one cannot explain away.

The Picture of Dorian Gray

Of course married life is merely a habit, a bad habit. But then one regrets the loss even of one's worst habits. Perhaps one regrets them the most. They are such an essential part of one's personality.

The Picture of Dorian Gray

All crime is vulgar, just as all vulgarity is crime.

The Picture of Dorian Gray

Crime belongs exclusively to the lower orders. I don't blame them in the smallest degree. I should fancy that crime was to them what art is to us, simply a method of procuring extraordinary sensations.

The Picture of Dorian Gray

Chapter 2

THE DUEL BETWEEN THE SEXES

Wilde's most commonly performed plays revolve round the relationships between men and women: courtship, marriage and illicit affairs. The courtships are light-hearted, as befits an age when premarital experience of the other sex was virtually non-existent and when courtship was many a woman's last opportunity to assert her independence. Marriage was not necessarily disastrous in Wilde's eyes – the initial few years of his marriage seem to have been happy – but involved more complex feelings and actions than some people imagined. His attitude to illicit affairs simply reflected the truth: that they were extremely hard on the women involved, while letting the men off entirely. Wilde clearly felt that women's position in society was wrongly inferior.

Men marry because they are tired; women, because they are curious; both are disappointed.

The Picture of Dorian Gray

A man can be happy with any woman, as long as he does not love her.

The Picture of Dorian Gray

I am not in favour of long engagements. They give people the opportunity of finding out each other's character before marriage, which I think is never advisable.

The Importance of Being Earnest

All women become like their mothers. That is their tragedy. No man does. That's his.

The Importance of Being Earnest

London is full of women who trust their husbands. One can always recognize them. They look so thoroughly unhappy.

Lady Windermere's Fan

Good heavens! How marriage ruins a man! It's as demoralizing as cigarettes, and far more expensive.

Lady Windermere's Fan

Well, there's nothing in the world like the devotion of a married woman. It's a thing no married man knows anything about.

Lady Windermere's Fan

She behaves as if she was beautiful. Most American women do. It is the secret of their charm.

The Picture of Dorian Gray

Lord Henry Wotton's views on marriage are quite monstrous, and I highly disapprove of them.

Letters

ALGERNON: Why is it that at a bachelor's establishment the servants invariably drink the champagne? I ask merely for information.

LANE: I attribute it to the superior quality of the wine, sir. I have often observed that in married households the champagne is rarely of a first-rate brand.

ALGERNON: Good heavens! Is marriage so demoralizing as that?

The Importance of Being Earnest

Women have no appreciation of good looks; at least, good women have not.

The Picture of Dorian Gray

Always! That is a dreadful word. It makes me shudder when I hear it. Women are so fond of using it. They spoil every romance by trying to make it last for ever. It is a meaningless word, too. The only difference between a caprice and a life-long passion is that the caprice lasts a little longer.

The Picture of Dorian Gray

Young men want to be faithful, and are not: old men want to be faithless, and cannot ...

The Picture of Dorian Gray

American girls are as clever at concealing their parents as English women are at concealing their past.

The Picture of Dorian Gray

... no woman is a genius. Women are a decorative sex. They never have anything to say, but they say it charmingly. Women represent the triumph of matter over mind, just as men represent the triumph of mind over morals.

The Picture of Dorian Gray

~ ❦ ~

Oh, there is only one real tragedy in a woman's life. The fact that her past is always her lover, and her future invariably her husband.

An Ideal Husband

~ ❦ ~

When a woman marries again it is because she detested her first husband. When a man marries again it is because he adored his first wife. Women try their luck; men risk theirs.

The Picture of Dorian Gray

Women love us for our defects. If we have enough of them they will forgive us everything, even our intellects.

The Picture of Dorian Gray

The amount of women in London who flirt with their own husbands is perfectly scandalous. It looks so bad. It is simply washing one's clean linen in public.

The Importance of Being Earnest

The only way to behave to a woman is to make love to her, if she is pretty, and to some one else, if she is plain.

The Importance of Being Earnest

Oh, I don't think I would care to catch a sensible man. I shouldn't know what to talk to him about.

The Importance of Being Earnest

... by persistently remaining single, a man converts himself into a permanent public temptation.

The Importance of Being Earnest

LADY WINDERMERE: Are all men bad?
DUCHESS OF BERWICK: Oh, all of them, my dear, all of them, without any exception. And they never grow any better. Men become old but they never become good.

Lady Windermere's Fan

Crying is the refuge of plain women but the ruin of pretty ones.

Lady Windermere's Fan

Between men and women there is no friendship possible. There is passion, enmity, worship, love, but no friendship.

Lady Windermere's Fan

When men give up saying what is charming, they give up thinking what is charming.

Lady Windermere's Fan

~❦~

Men are such cowards. They outrage every law of the world, and are afraid of the world's tongue.

Lady Windermere's Fan

~❦~

Wicked women bother one. Good women bore one. That is the only difference between them.

Lady Windermere's Fan

~❦~

It is not customary in England … for a young lady to speak with such enthusiasm of any person of the opposite sex. English women conceal their feelings till after they are married. They show them then.

A Woman of No Importance

LADY STUTFIELD: The world was made for men and not for women.

MRS ALLONBY: Oh, don't say that, Lady Stutfield. We have a much better time than they have. There are far more things forbidden to us than are forbidden to them.

A Woman of No Importance

The growing influence of women is the one reassuring thing in our political life ... Women are always on the side of morality, public and private.

A Woman of No Importance

Curious thing, plain women are always jealous of their husbands, beautiful women never are! ... Beautiful women never have time. They are always too occupied in being jealous of other people's husbands.

A Woman of No Importance

Twenty years of romance make a woman look like a ruin; but twenty years of marriage make her something like a public building.

A Woman of No Importance

Nothing spoils a romance so much as a sense of humour in the woman.

A Woman of No Importance

Men always want to be a woman's first love. That is their clumsy vanity.

A Woman of No Importance

I don't think there is a woman in the world who would not be a little flattered if one made love to her. It is that which makes women so irresistibly adorable.

A Woman of No Importance

LORD ILLINGWORTH: The Book of Life begins with a man and a woman in a garden.

MRS ALLONBY: It ends with Revelations.

A Woman of No Importance

LADY STUTFIELD: Yes; men persecute us dreadfully, don't they?

MRS ALLONBY: Persecute us? I wish they did ... The annoying thing is that the wretches can be perfectly happy without us.

A Woman of No Importance

One should never trust a woman who tells one her real age. A woman who would tell one that, would tell one anything.

A Woman of No Importance

More marriages are ruined nowadays by the common sense of the husband than by anything else. How can a woman be expected to be happy with a man who insists on treating her as if she was a perfectly rational being?

A Woman of No Importance

He should never run down other pretty women. That would show he had no taste, or make one suspect that he had too much. No; he should be nice about them all, but say that somehow they don't attract him.

A Woman of No Importance

[The Ideal Man] He should persistently compromise us in public and treat us with absolute respect when we are alone. And yet he should be always ready to have a perfectly terrible scene, whenever we want one, and to become miserable, absolutely miserable, at a moment's notice, and to overwhelm us with just reproaches in less than twenty minutes, and to be positively violent at the end of half an hour, and to leave us for ever at a quarter to eight, when we have to go and dress for dinner ... and after a whole dreadful week ... if his conduct has been quite irreproachable, and one has behaved really badly to him, he should be allowed to admit that he has been entirely in the wrong, and when he has admitted that, it becomes a woman's duty to forgive, and one can do it all over again from the beginning, with variations.

A Woman of No Importance

LADY CAROLINE: There are a great many things you haven't got in America, I am told.

MISS WORSLEY: They say you have no ruins and no curiosities.

MRS ALLONBY: What nonsense! They have their mothers and their manners.

A Woman of No Importance

Oh! Talk to every woman as if you loved her, and to every man as if he bored you, and at the end of your first season you will have the reputation of possessing the most perfect social tact.

A Woman of No Importance

Our husbands never appreciate anything in us. We have to go to others for that!

An Ideal Husband

The history of women is the history of the worst form of tyranny the world has ever known. The tyranny of the weak over the strong. It is the only tyranny that lasts.

A Woman of No Importance

JACK: . . . Cecily and Gwendolen are perfectly certain to be extremely great friends. I'll bet you anything you like that half an hour after they have met, they will be calling each other sister.

ALGERNON: Women only do that when they have called each other a lot of other things first.

The Importance of Being Earnest

Well, she wore far too much rouge last night, and not quite enough clothes. That is always the sign of despair in a woman.

An Ideal Husband

Women think that they are making ideals of men.
What they are making of us are false idols merely.

An Ideal Husband

LORD GORING: I am glad you have called. I am going
to give you some good advice.
MRS CHEVELY: Oh! pray don't. One should never give
a woman anything that she can't wear in the evening.

An Ideal Husband

… we women never know
Our lovers till they leave us.

The Duchess of Padua

Women are not meant to judge us, but to forgive us
when we need forgiveness.

An Ideal Husband

Too much experience is a dangerous thing. Pray have a cigarette. Half the pretty women in London smoke cigarettes. Personally I prefer the other half.

An Ideal Husband

~❧~

I don't see why a man should think he is pleasing a woman enormously when he says to her a whole heap of things that he doesn't mean.

Lady Windermere's Fan

~❧~

LADY WINDERMERE: Because the husband is vile – should the wife be vile also?

LORD DARLINGTON: Vileness is a terrible word, Lady Windermere.

LADY WINDERMERE: It is a terrible thing, Lord Darlington.

Lady Windermere's Fan

Now I know that all men are monsters. The only thing to do is to feed the wretches well. A good cook does wonders ...

Lady Windermere's Fan

That is the worst of women. They always want one to be good. And if we are good, when they meet us, they don't love us at all. They like to find us quite irretrievably bad, and to leave us quite unattractively good.

Lady Windermere's Fan

It's most dangerous nowadays for a husband to pay any attention to his wife in public. It always makes people think that he beats her when they're alone. The world has grown so suspicious of anything that looks like a happy married life.

Lady Windermere's Fan

... I want you to take my husband with you. He has been so attentive lately, that he has become a perfect nuisance. He'll dance attendance upon her as long as she lets him, and won't bother me. I assure you, women of that kind are most useful. They form the basis of other people's marriages.

Lady Windermere's Fan

Egad! I might be married to her; she treats me with such demmed indifference.

Lady Windermere's Fan

LORD DARLINGTON: This woman has purity and innocence. She has everything we men have lost.
CECIL GRAHAM: My dear fellow, what on earth should we men do going about with purity and innocence? A carefully thought-out buttonhole is much more effective.

Lady Windermere's Fan

HESTER: Do you, in England, allow no friendship to exist between a young man and a young girl?

LADY CAROLINE: We think it very inadvisable.

A Woman of No Importance

LADY CAROLINE: … These American girls carry off all the good matches. Why can't they stay in their country? They are always telling us it is the Paradise of women.

LORD ILLINGWORTH: It is, Lady Caroline. That is why, like Eve, they are so extremely anxious to get out of it.

A Woman of No Importance

Now, I have never regarded women as a toy. Woman is the intellectual helpmeet of man in public as in private life. Without her we should forget the true ideals.

A Woman of No Importance

Femininity is the quality I admire most in women.

A Woman of No Importance

MRS ALLONBY: Twenty years of romance! Is there such a thing?

LORD ILLINGWORTH: Not in our day. Women have become too brilliant. Nothing spoils a romance so much as a sense of humour in the woman.

MRS ALLONBY: Or the want of it in the man.

A Woman of No Importance

MRS ALLONBY: She is a Puritan besides –

LORD ILLINGWORTH: Ah, that is inexcusable. I don't mind plain women being Puritans. It is the only excuse they have for being plain. But she is decidedly pretty.

A Woman of No Importance

LORD ILLINGWORTH: What do you call a bad man?

MRS ALLONBY: The sort of man who admires innocence.

LORD ILLINGWORTH: And a bad woman?

MRS ALLONBY: Oh! the sort of woman a man never gets tired of.

A Woman of No Importance

LORD ILLINGWORTH: Don't you know that I always succeed in whatever I try?

MRS ALLONBY: I am sorry to hear it. We women adore failures. They lean on us.

A Woman of No Importance

MRS ALLONBY: It is such a strain keeping men up to the mark. They are always trying to escape from us.

A Woman of No Importance

MRS ALLONBY: ... All men are married women's property. That is the only true definition of what married women's property really is. But we don't belong to anyone.

A Woman of No Importance

LADY STUTFIELD: Oh, I think one can always know at once whether a man has home claims upon his life or not. I have noticed a very, very sad expression in the eyes of so many married men.

MRS ALLONBY: Ah, all I have noticed is that they are horribly tedious when they are good husbands, and abominably conceited when they are not.

A Woman of No Importance

MRS ALLONBY: ... It is only fair to tell you beforehand he has got no conversation at all.

LADY STUTFIELD: I adore silent men.

MRS ALLONBY: Oh, Ernest isn't silent. He talks the whole time. But he has got no conversation. What he talks about I don't know. I haven't listened to him for years.

A Woman of No Importance

~ ⟨⟩ ~

Nothing is so aggravating as calmness. There is something positively brutal about the good temper of most modern men. I wonder we women stand it as well as we do.

A Woman of No Importance

~ ⟨⟩ ~

Oh, women have become so highly educated ... that nothing should surprise us nowadays, except happy marriages. They apparently are getting remarkably rare.

A Woman of No Importance

Man, poor, awkward, reliable, necessary man belongs to a sex that has been rational for millions and millions of years. He can't help himself. It is in his race. The History of Woman is very different. We have always been picturesque protests against the very existence of common sense. We saw its dangers from the first.

A Woman of No Importance

GERALD: It is very difficult to understand women, is it not?
LORD ILLINGWORTH: You should never try to understand them. Women are pictures. Men are problems. If you want to know what a woman really means – which, by the way, is always a dangerous thing to do – look at her, don't listen to her.

A Woman of No Importance

Women are a fascinatingly wilful sex. Every woman is a rebel, and usually in wild revolt against herself.

A Woman of No Importance

GERALD: But don't you think one can be happy when one is married?

LORD ILLINGWORTH: Perfectly happy. But the happiness of a married man, my dear Gerald, depends on the people he has not married.

A Woman of No Importance

One should always be in love. That is the reason one should never marry.

A Woman of No Importance

MRS ALLONBY: There is a beautiful moon tonight.

LORD ILLINGWORTH: Let us go and look at it. To look at anything that is inconstant is charming nowadays.

MRS ALLONBY: You have your looking-glass.

LORD ILLINGWORTH: It is unkind. It merely shows me my wrinkles.

MRS ALLONBY: Mine is better behaved. It never tells me the truth.

LORD ILLINGWORTH: Then it is in love with you.

A Woman of No Importance

LORD ILLINGWORTH: I was very young at the time. We men know life too early.

MRS ARBUTHNOT: And we women know life too late. That is the difference between men and women.

A Woman of No Importance

I don't know that women are always rewarded for being charming. I think they are usually punished for it! Certainly, more women grow old nowadays through the faithfulness of their admirers than through anything else! At least that is the only way I can account for the terribly haggard look of most of your pretty women in London!

An Ideal Husband

… the strength of women comes from the fact that psychology cannot explain us. Men can be analysed, women … merely adored.

An Ideal Husband

Oh! I don't care about the London season! It is too matrimonial. People are either hunting for husbands, or hiding from them.

An Ideal Husband

~·{♣·~

We have married perfect husbands, and we are well punished for it.

An Ideal Husband

~·{♣·~

English men always get so romantic after a meal, and that bores me dreadfully.

An Ideal Husband

~·{♣·~

I have often observed that the Season as it goes on produces a kind of softening of the brain. However, I think anything is better than high intellectual pressure. That is the most unbecoming thing there is. It makes the noses of the young girls so particularly large. And there is nothing so difficult to marry as a large nose; men don't like them.

An Ideal Husband

... men can love what is beneath them — things unworthy, stained, dishonoured. We women worship when we love; and when we lose our worship, we lose everything.

An Ideal Husband

But no man should have a secret from his own wife. She invariably finds it out. Women have a wonderful instinct about things. They can discover everything except the obvious.

An Ideal Husband

The higher education of men is what I should like to see. Men need it so sadly.

An Ideal Husband

I don't think man has much capacity for development. He has got as far as he can, and that is not far, is it?

An Ideal Husband

It is the growth of the moral sense in women that makes marriage such a hopeless, one-sided institution.

An Ideal Husband

LORD CAVERSHAM: No woman, plain or pretty, has any common sense at all, sir. Common sense is the privilege of our sex.
LORD GORING: Quite so. And we men are so self-sacrificing that we never use it, do we, father?

An Ideal Husband

I suppose that when a man has once loved a woman, he will do anything for her, except continue to love her?

An Ideal Husband

... women are never disarmed by compliments. Men always are. That is the difference between the two sexes.

An Ideal Husband

... if we men married the women we deserved, we should have a very bad time of it.

An Ideal Husband

Women are not meant to judge us but to forgive us when we need forgiveness.

An Ideal Husband

An ideal husband! Oh, I don't think I should like that. It sounds like something in the next world.

An Ideal Husband

I have only been married once. That was in consequence of a misunderstanding between myself and a young person.

The Importance of Being Earnest

… girls never marry the men they flirt with. Girls don't think it right … It accounts for the extraordinary number of bachelors that one sees all over the place.

The Importance of Being Earnest

ALGERNON: You don't seem to realize, that in married life three is company and two is none.

JACK: That, my dear young friend, is the theory that the corrupt French Drama has been propounding for the last fifty years.

ALGERNON: Yes; and that the happy English home has proved in half the time.

The Importance of Being Earnest

JACK: ... It's perfectly easy to be cynical.

ALGERNON: My dear fellow, it isn't easy to be anything nowadays. There's such a lot of beastly competition about.

The Importance of Being Earnest

... ever since I met you I have admired you more than any girl ... I have ever met since ... I met you.

The Importance of Being Earnest

I have always been of the opinion that a man who desires to get married should know either everything or nothing.

The Importance of Being Earnest

My dear fellow, the truth isn't quite the sort of thing one tells to a nice, sweet, refined girl. What extraordinary ideas you have about the way to behave to a woman.

The Importance of Being Earnest

CECILY: Miss Prism says that all good looks are a snare.

ALGERNON: They are a snare that every sensible man would like to be caught in.

The Importance of Being Earnest

I don't quite like women who are interested in philanthropic work. I think it is so forward of them.

The Importance of Being Earnest

London society is full of women of the very highest birth who have, of their own free choice, remained thirty-five for years.

The Importance of Being Earnest

… but nowadays everybody is jealous of everyone else, except, of course, husband and wife.

Letters

You seem to forget that I am married, and the one charm of marriage is that it makes a life of deception absolutely necessary for both parties. I never know where my wife is, and my wife never knows what I am doing. When we meet ... we tell each other the most absurd stories with the most serious faces. My wife is very good at it — much better, in fact, than I am. She never gets confused over her dates and I always do.

The Picture of Dorian Gray

Ordinary women never appeal to one's imagination. They are limited to their century. No glamour ever transfigures them. One knows their minds as easily as one knows their bonnets. One can always find them. There is no mystery in any of them.

The Picture of Dorian Gray

Women defend themselves by attacking, just as they attack by sudden and strange surrenders.

The Picture of Dorian Gray

Besides, every experience is of value, and, whatever one may say against marriage, it is certainly an experience.

The Picture of Dorian Gray

~ 🔹 ~

As for marriage, ... there are other and more interesting bonds between men and women. I will certainly encourage them. They have the charm of being fashionable.

The Picture of Dorian Gray

~ 🔹 ~

"Women are wonderfully practical," murmured Lord Henry – "much more practical than we are. In situations of that kind we often forget to say anything about marriage, and they always remind us."

The Picture of Dorian Gray

"You must admit, Harry, that women give to men the very gold of their lives."

"Possibly," he sighed, "but they invariably want it back in such very small change. That is the worry. Women, as some witty Frenchman once put it, inspire us with the desire to do masterpieces, and always prevent us from carrying them out.

The Picture of Dorian Gray

There is always something ridiculous about the emotions of people one has ceased to love.

The Picture of Dorian Gray

Besides, women were better suited to bear sorrow than men. They lived on their emotions. They thought only of their emotions. When they took loves, it was merely to have someone with whom they could have scenes.

The Picture of Dorian Gray

... the only way a woman can ever reform a man is by boring him so completely that he loses all possible interest in life.

The Picture of Dorian Gray

That awful memory of woman! What a fearful thing it is! And what an utter intellectual stagnation it reveals! One should absorb the colour of life, but one should never remember its details. Details are always vulgar.

The Picture of Dorian Gray

The one charm of the past is that it is the past. But women never know when the curtain has fallen. They always want a sixth act, and as soon as the interest of the play is entirely over they propose to continue it. If they were allowed their own way, every comedy would have a tragic ending, and every tragedy would culminate in farce.

The Picture of Dorian Gray

He was dreadfully short-sighted, and there is no pleasure in taking in a husband who never sees anything.

The Picture of Dorian Gray

I like men who have a future, and women who have a
past.

The Picture of Dorian Gray

She is very clever, too clever for a woman. She lacks
the indefinable charm of weakness. It is the feet of
clay that make the gold of the image precious.

The Picture of Dorian Gray

We women, as someone says, love with our ears, just as
you men love with your eyes, if you ever love at all.

The Picture of Dorian Gray

How fond women are of doing dangerous things! ... It is one of the qualities in them that I admire most. A woman will flirt with anybody in the world as long as other people are looking on.

The Picture of Dorian Gray

Chapter 3

ART FOR ART'S SAKE, AND BEYOND

Wilde was keen on a school of thought that held that beauty, especially as rendered by art, is the highest thing in life. Known as the Aesthetic School, its ideas are often summarized as "Art for Art's sake." Its supporters were generally regarded as decadent by society, partly because writers such as Wilde discussed the "immorality" of art (now we would probably use the term "amoral"). Also, many of its best known characters, such as Wilde's Dorian Gray and Huysmans's entirely indolent young anti-hero, led truly dissolute lives (although nowhere is the actual form of this dissolution described – late Victorian England was priggish but prurient), and this was seen as a reflection of the characters of the authors. As Wilde points out, they might as well have called Shakespeare mad because he wrote King Lear. Aestheticism was seen as superficial and rarefied to its detractors, partly because it rejected the Romantic worship of Nature.

... Beauty is a form of Genius – is higher, indeed, than Genius, as it needs no explanation.

The Picture of Dorian Gray

The pleasure that one has in creating a work of art is a purely personal pleasure, and it is for the sake of this pleasure that one creates. The artist works with his eye on the object. Nothing else interests him. What people are likely to say does not even occur to him. He is fascinated by what he has in hand. He is indifferent to others. I write because it gives me the greatest possible artistic pleasure to write. If my work pleases the few, I am gratified. If it does not, it causes me no pain. As for the mob, I have no desire to be a popular novelist. It is far too easy.

Letters

Success is a science; if you have the conditions, you get the result. Art is the mathematical result of the emotional desire for beauty. If it is not thought out, it is nothing.

Letters

Art is useless because its aim is simply to create a mood. It is not meant to instruct, or to influence action in any way. It is superbly sterile, and the note of its pleasure is sterility. If the contemplation of a work of art is followed by activity of any kind, the work is either of a very second-rate order, or the spectator has failed to realize the complete artistic impression.

Letters

The proper school to learn art in is not Life but Art.

The Decay of Lying

A work of art is useless as a flower is useless. A flower blossoms for its own joy. We gain a moment of joy by looking at it ... Of course man may sell the flower and so make it useful to him, but this has nothing to do with the flower. It is not part of its essence. It is accidental. It is a misuse.

Letters

～⁛～

No artist recognises any standard of beauty but that which is suggested by his own temperament. The artist seeks to realize in a certain material his immaterial idea of beauty, and thus to transform an idea into an ideal. That is the way an artist makes things. That is why an artist makes things. The artist has no other object in making things.

Letters

～⁛～

What the artist is always looking for is that mode of existence in which soul and body are one and indivisible: in which the outward is expressive of the inward: in which Form reveals.

Letters

Truth in Art is the unity of a thing with itself: the outward rendered expressive of the inward: the soul made incarnate: the body instinct with spirit.

Letters

For the artistic life is simple self-development. Humility in the artist is his frank acceptance of all experiences, just as Love in the artist is simply that sense of Beauty that reveals to the world its body and its soul.

Letters

Every single work of art is the fulfilment of a prophecy. For every work of art is the conversion of an idea into an image.

Letters

The sitter is merely the accident, the occasion. It is not he who is revealed by the painter; it is rather the painter who, on the coloured canvas, reveals himself.

The Picture of Dorian Gray

Art never expresses anything but itself. It has an independent life, just as Thought has, and develops purely on its own lines. It is not necessarily realistic in an age of realism, nor spiritual in an age of faith. So far from being the creation of its time, it is usually in direct opposition to it, and the only history that it preserves for us is the history of its own progress.

The Decay of Lying

… when a thing is useless it should be made beautiful, otherwise it has no reason for existing at all.

Letters

Art finds her own perfection within, and not outside of, herself. She is not to be judged by an external standard of resemblance. She is a veil, rather than a mirror.

The Decay of Lying

～🖤～

Nature is a foolish place to look for inspiration in, but a charming one in which to forget one ever had any.

Letters

～🖤～

A thing in Nature becomes much lovelier if it reminds us of a thing in Art, but a thing in Art gains no real beauty through reminding us of a thing in Nature. The primary aesthetic impression of a work of art borrows nothing from recognition or resemblance … they are not part of a real aesthetic impression at all, and the constant preoccupation with subject-matter that characterizes nearly all our English art-criticism is what makes our art-criticism, especially as regards literature, so sterile, so profitless, so much beside the mark, and of such curiously little account.

Letters

... the more we study Art, the less we care for Nature.

The Decay of Lying

~⚜~

A really well-made buttonhole is the only link between Art and Nature.

"Phrases and Philosophies for the Use of the Young"

~⚜~

Life imitates Art ... Life in fact is the mirror, and Art the reality.

The Decay of Lying

~⚜~

An artist ... has no ethical sympathies at all. Virtue and wickedness are to him simply what the colours on his palette are to the painter ... Iago may be morally horrible and Imogen stainlessly pure. Shakespeare ... had as much delight in creating the one as he had in creating the other.

Letters

For if a work of art is rich, and vital, and complete, those who have artistic instincts will see its beauty, and those to whom ethics appeal more strongly than aesthetics will see its moral lesson. It will fill the cowardly with terror, and the unclean will see in it their own shame. It will be to each man what he is himself. It is the spectator, and not life, that art really mirrors.

Letters

If a man sees the artistic beauty of a thing, he will probably care very little for its ethical import. If his temperament is more susceptible to ethical than to aesthetic influences, he will be blind to questions of style, treatment and the like. It takes a Goethe to see a work of art fully, completely, and perfectly …

Letters

When criticism becomes in England a real art, as it should be, and when none but those of artistic instinct and artistic cultivation is allowed to write about works of art, artists will no doubt read criticisms with a certain amount of intellectual interest.

Letters

The critic has to educate the public; the artist has to educate the critic.

Letters

The public has always, and in every age, been badly brought up. They are continually asking Art to be popular, to please their want of taste, to flatter their absurd vanity, to tell them what they have been told before ...

The Soul of Man under Socialism

To call an artist morbid because he deals with morbidity as his subject-matter is as silly as if one called Shakespeare mad because he wrote King Lear.

The Soul of Man under Socialism

… and as for borrowing Mr Whistler's ideas about art, the only thoroughly original ideas I have ever heard him express have had reference to his own superiority over painters greater than himself.

Letters

… his work was that curious mixture of bad painting and good intentions that always entitles a man to be called a representative British artist.

The Picture of Dorian Gray

Modern pictures are, no doubt, delightful to look at. At least, some of them are. But they are quite impossible to live with; they are too clever, too assertive, too intellectual. Their meaning is too obvious, and their method too clearly defined. One exhausts what they have to say in a very short time, and they become as tedious as one's relations.

The Critic as Artist

[Of Shelley] If the English had realized what a great poet he really was, they would have fallen on him with tooth and nail, and made his life as unbearable to him as they possibly could.

The Soul of Man under Socialism

… the moment that an artist takes notice of what other people want, and tries to supply the demand, he ceases to be an artist …

The Soul of Man under Socialism

... Art should never try to be popular. The public should try to make itself artistic.

The Soul of Man under Socialism

~·◦·~

In England, the arts that have escaped best are the arts in which the public take no interest. Poetry is an instance ...

The Soul of Man under Socialism

~·◦·~

In Art, the public accept what has been because they cannot alter it, not because they appreciate it. They swallow their classics whole, and never taste them.

The Soul of Man under Socialism

~·◦·~

... the public make use of the classics of a country as a means of checking the progress of Art. They degrade the classics into authorities.

The Soul of Man under Socialism

... no artist expects grace from the vulgar mind, or style from the suburban intellect.

The Soul of Man under Socialism

The work of art is to dominate the spectator: the spectator is not to dominate the work of art.

The Soul of Man under Socialism

Most of our modern portrait painters are doomed to absolute oblivion. They never paint what they see. They paint what the public sees, and the public never sees anything.

The Decay of Lying

The fact is that we look back on the ages entirely through the medium of art, and art, very fortunately, has never once told us the truth.

The Decay of Lying

... we have lost the faculty of giving lovely names to things. Names are everything. That is the reason I hate vulgar realism in literature. The man who could call a spade a spade should be compelled to use one.

The Picture of Dorian Gray

Why should clogs be despised? Much art has been expended on clogs. They have been made of lovely woods, and delicately inlaid with ivory, and with mother-of-pearl. A clog might be a dream of beauty, and if not too high or heavy, most comfortable also.

Letters

The truth is rarely pure and never simple. Modern life would be very tedious if it were either, and modern literature a complete impossibility!

The Importance of Being Earnest

The only form of lying that is absolutely beyond reproach is lying for its own sake, and the highest development of this is, as we have already pointed out, lying in Art.

The Decay of Lying

In matters of grave importance, style, not sincerity, is the vital thing.

The Importance of Being Earnest

Nowadays people seem to look on life as a speculation. It is not a speculation. It is a sacrament. Its ideal is Love. Its purification is Sacrifice.

Lady Windermere's Fan

All bad art comes from returning to Life and Nature, and elevating them into ideals. Life and Nature may sometimes be used as part of Art's rough material, but before they are of any real service to Art they must be translated into artistic conventions. The moment Art surrenders its imaginative medium it surrenders everything.

The Decay of Lying

Spirit of Beauty! Tarry still a-while,
They are not dead, thine ancient votaries; …

Who for thy sake would give their manlihood
And consecrate their being, I at least
Have done so, made thy lips my daily food,
And in thy temples found a goodlier feast
Than this starved age can give me, spite of all
Its new-found creeds so sceptical and dogmatical …

But they [true artists] are few, and all romance has
    flown,
And men can prophesy about the sun,
And lecture on his arrows – how, alone,
Through a waste void the soulless atoms run,

How far from each tree its weeping nymph has fled,
And that no more 'mid English reeds a Naiad shows
   her head.

Methinks these new Actaeons boast too soon
That they have spied on beauty; what if we
Have analysed the rainbow, robbed the moon
Of her most ancient, chastest mystery,
Shall I, the last Endymion, lose all hope
Because rude eyes peer at my mistress through a tele-
   scope!

What profit if this scientific age
Burst through our gates with all its retinue
Of modern miracles! Can it assuage
One lover's breaking heart? What can it do
To make one life more beautiful, one day
More godlike in its period? But now the age of Clay

Returns in horrid cycle, and the earth
Hath borne again a noisy progeny
Of ignorant Titans, whose ungodly birth
Hurls them against the august hierarchy
Which sat upon Olympus …
                     "The Garden of Eros"

One should sympathize with the joy, the beauty, the colour of life. The less said about life's sores the better.

A Woman of No Importance

… nowadays the selection of colours and furniture has quite taken the place of the cases of conscience of the middle ages, and usually involves quite as much remorse.

Letters

… the Muses are as often to be met with in our English fields as they ever were by Castaly, or Helicon.

Letters

… all art requires solitude as its companion.

Letters

Believe me, I would as lief judge of the strength and splendour of the sun and sea by the dust that dances in the beam and the bubble that breaks on the wave, as take the petty and profitless vulgarity of one or two insignificant towns as any test or standard of the real spirit of a sane, strong and simple people, or allow it to affect my respect for the many noble men and women whom it has been my privilege in this great country to know.

Letters

… all brilliant people should cross each other's cycles, like some of the nicest planets.

Letters

Youth being so glorious, art so godlike, and the very world about us so full of beautiful things, and things worthy of reverence, and things honourable, how should one stop to listen to the lucubrations of a literary gamin, to the brawling and mouthing of a man whose praise would be as insolent as his slander is impotent, or to the irresponsible and irrepressible chatter of the professionally unproductive.

Letters

In every city they start schools of decorative art after my visit, and set on foot public museums, getting my advice about the choice of objects and the nature of the building. And the artists treat me like a young god.

Letters

I have met [US] miners: they are big-booted, red-shirted, yellow-bearded and delightful ruffians ... I secretly believe they read up Bret Harte privately; they were certainly almost as real as his miners, and quite as pleasant. With my usual passion for personality I entertained them, and had a delightful time, though on my making some mention of early Florentine art they unanimously declared they could neither "trump or follow it."

Letters

The amazement of the miners when they saw that art and appetite could go hand in had knew no bounds; when I lit a long cigar they cheered till the silver fell in dust from the roof on our plates and when I quaffed a cocktail without flinching, they unanimously pronounced me in their grand simple way "a bully boy with no glass eye" – artless and spontaneous praise which touched me more than the pompous panegyrics of literary critics ever did or could.

Letters

I feel an irresistible desire to wander, and go to Japan, where I will pass my youth, sitting under an almond tree in white blossom, drinking amber tea out of a blue cup, and looking at a landscape without perspective.

Letters

But I can't travel without Balzac and Gautier, and they take up so much room: and as long as I enjoy talking nonsense to flowers and children I am not afraid of the depraved luxury of a hat-box.

Letters

The dream of the sculptor is cold and silent in the marble, the painter's vision immobile on the canvas.

Letters

As regards dialogue, you can produce tragic effects by introducing comedy. A laugh in an audience does not destroy terror, but, by relieving it, aids it. Never be afraid that by raising a laugh you destroy tragedy. On the contrary you intensify it.

Letters

… the best work of art in our days is that which combines classic grace with absolute reality …

Letters

I am deeply distressed to hear that the tuberose is so called from its being a "lumpy flower." It is not at all lumpy, and, even if it were, no poet should be heartless enough to say so. Henceforth there really must be two derivations for every word, one for the poet and one for the scientist … On the roots of verbs Philology must be allowed to speak, but on the roots of flowers she must keep silence. We cannot allow her to dig up Parnassus [home of the Muses].

Letters

Books, I fancy, may be conveniently divided into three classes: 1. Books to read ... 2. Books to re-read, such as Plato and Keats: in the sphere of poetry, the masters not the minstrels; in the sphere of philosophy, the seers not the savants. 3. Books not to read at all, such as ... all John Stuart Mill except the Essay on Liberty, all Voltaire's plays without any exception ... all argumentative books and all books that try to prove anything.

The third class is by far the most important. To tell people what to read is, as a rule, either useless or harmful; for the appreciation of literature is a question of temperament not of teaching; to Parnassus there is no primer and nothing that one can learn is ever worth learning. But to tell people what not to read is a very different matter ...

Letters

I do not suppose that the criminal and illiterate classes ever read anything except newspapers.

Letters

Your critic then, sir, commits the absolutely unpardonable crime of trying to confuse the artist with his subject-matter. For this, sir, there is no excuse at all. Of one who is the greatest figure in the world's literature since Greek days Keats remarked that he had as much pleasure conceiving the evil as he had in conceiving the good ... One stands remote from one's subject-matter. One creates it, and one contemplates it. The further away the subject-matter is, the more freely can the artist work.

Letters

I am afraid that writing to newspapers has a deteriorating influence on style. People get violent, and abusive, and lose all sense of proportion, when they enter that curious journalistic arena in which the race is always to the noisiest.

Letters

The coat, then, of next season, will be an exquisite colour-note, and have also a great psychological value. It will emphasise the serious and thoughtful side of a man's character. One will be able to discern a man's views of life by the colour he selects … The imagination will concentrate itself on the waistcoat. Waistcoats will show whether a man can admire poetry or not.

Letters

But if one is to behave badly, it is better to be bad in a becoming dress than in one that is unbecoming …

Letters

As things are at present, the criticisms of ordinary newspapers are of no interest whatsoever, except in so far as the display in its crudest form the extraordinary Boeotianism of a country that has produced some Athenians, and in which other Athenians have come to dwell.

Letters

How strange to live in a land where the worship of beauty and the passion of love are considered infamous.

Letters

The Philistine element in life is not the failure to understand Art. Charming people such as fishermen, shepherds, ploughboys, peasants and the like know nothing about Art, and are the very salt of the earth. He is the Philistine who upholds and aids the heavy, cumbrous, blind mechanical forces of Society, and who does not recognize the dynamic force when he meets it either in a man or a movement.

Letters

Language requires to be tuned, like a violin: and just as too many or too few vibrations in the voice of the singer or the trembling of the string will make the note false, so too much or too little in words will spoil the message.

Letters

Whatever is first in feeling comes always last in form.

Letters

I have a strange longing for the great simple primeval things, such as the Sea, to me no less of a mother than the Earth. It seems to me that we all look at Nature too much, and live with her too little. I discern great sanity in the Greek attitude. They never chattered about sunsets, or discussed whether the shadows on the grass were really mauve or not. But they saw that the sea was for the swimmer, and the sand for the feet of the runner. They loved the trees for the shadow that they cast, and the forest for its silence at noon.

Letters

There is not a single colour hidden away in the chalice of a flower, or the curve of a shell, to which, by some subtle sympathy with the very soul of things, my nature does not answer.

Letters

I need not remind you that mere expression is to an artist the supreme and only mode of life. It is by utterance that we live.

Letters

I am not a scrap ashamed of having been in prison. I am horribly ashamed of the materialism of the life that brought me there. It was quite unworthy of an artist.

Letters

One can really ... be far more subjective in an objective form than in any other way. If I were asked of myself as a dramatist, I would say that my unique position was that I had taken the Drama, the most objective form known to art, and made it as personal a mode of expression as the Lyric or the Sonnet, while enriching the characterization of the stage, and enlarging — at any rate in the case of Salome — its artistic horizon.

Letters

The egoistic note is, of course, and always has been to me, the primal and ultimate note of modern art, but to be an Egoist one must have an Ego. It is not everyone who says "I", "I" who can enter into the Kingdom of Art.

Letters

I love the last words of anything: the end in art is the beginning.

Letters

I have a wild desire for the sea. I feel that water purifies, and that in nature there is, for me at any rate, healing power.

Letters

I know simply that a life of definite and studied materialism, and a philosophy of appetite and cynicism, and a cult of sensual and senseless ease, are bad things for an artist: they narrow the imagination and dull the more delicate sensibilities.

Letters

When one uses the words poetry and prose, one is merely referring to certain technical modes of word-music, melody and harmony one might say, though they are not exclusive terms …

Letters

The public is largely influenced by the look of a book. So are we all. It is the only artistic thing about the public.

Letters

I don't think I shall ever write again: la joie de vivre is gone, and that, with will-power, is the basis of art.

Letters

Peace is as requisite to the artist as to the saint ...

Letters

Neither in Greek nor in Gothic art is there any pose. Posing was invented by bad portrait-painters, and the first person who ever posed was a stockbroker, and he has gone on ever since.

Letters

It is very curious the connection between Faith and bad art ...

Letters

The artist is the creator of beautiful things.

To reveal art and conceal the artist is art's aim.

The critic is he who can translate into another
manner or a new material his impression of beautiful things.

The highest, as the lowest, form of criticism is a mode
of autobiography.

Those who find ugly meanings in beautiful things are
corrupt without being charming. This is a fault.

Those who find beautiful meanings in beautiful
things are the cultivated. For these there is hope.

They are the elect to whom beautiful things mean only
Beauty.

There is no such thing as a moral or an immoral book.
Books are well written, or badly written. That is all.

The nineteenth-century dislike of Realism is the rage
of Caliban seeing his own face in a glass.

The nineteenth-century dislike of Romanticism is the
rage of Caliban not seeing his own face in the glass.

The Picture of Dorian Gray (preface)

No artist desires to prove anything. Even things that are true can be proved.

The Picture of Dorian Gray

We can forgive a man for making a useful thing as long as he does not admire it. The only excuse for making a useless thing is that one admires it intensely.

The Picture of Dorian Gray

We live in an age when men treat art as if it were meant to be a form of autobiography. We have lost the abstract sense of beauty.

The Picture of Dorian Gray

The aim of life is self-development. To realize one's nature perfectly — that is what each of us is here for. People are afraid of themselves, nowadays. They have forgotten the highest of all duties, the duty that one owes to one's self.

The Picture of Dorian Gray

~❧~

Music had stirred him like that. Music had troubled him many times. But music was not articulate. It was not a new world, but rather another chaos, that it created in us. Words! Mere words! How terrible they were! How clear, and vivid and cruel! One could not escape from them. And yet what a subtle magic there was in them! They seemed to be able to give a plastic form to formless things, and to have a music of their own as sweet as that of viola or of lute. Mere words! Was there anything so real as words?

The Picture of Dorian Gray

... the costume of the nineteenth century is detestable. It is so sombre, so depressing. Sin is the only real colour-element left in modern life.

The Picture of Dorian Gray

Behind every exquisite thing that existed, there was something tragic. Worlds had to be in travail, that the meanest flower might blow.

The Picture of Dorian Gray

But there is no literary public in England for anything except newspapers, primers, and encyclopaedias. Of all the people in the world the English have the least sense of the beauty of literature.

The Picture of Dorian Gray

I never talk during music, at least, during good music. If one hears bad music, it is one's duty to drown it in conversation.

The Picture of Dorian Gray

Most people become bankrupt through having invested too heavily in the prose of life. To have ruined one's self over poetry is an honour.

The Picture of Dorian Gray

He had that dislike of being stared at which comes on geniuses late in life, and never leaves the common-place.

The Picture of Dorian Gray

It often seems to me that art conceals the artist far more completely than it ever reveals him.

The Picture of Dorian Gray

Fashion, by which what is really fantastic becomes for a moment universal, and Dandyism, which, in its own way, is an attempt to assert the absolute modernity of beauty, had, of course, their fascination for him.

The Picture of Dorian Gray

Chapter 4

THE ARTIST AS PHILOSOPHER

*Wilde was not just the producer of an apparently inex-
haustible stream of wit. Much of his wit says more than sits
on the surface, and he also wrote several essays whose
content is philosophical. Wilde was extremely well-read
and highly educated, having been to university in Dublin
and Oxford, where he gained a double first in Classics. He
read extremely widely in ancient Greek drama and philosophy – Plato and Aristotle, for example – and in classical
verse. He was aware of the injustices of the world, more
keenly so during and after his time of imprisonment. As
with all his writing, the lightness of style often masks the
seriousness of content.*

"Know thyself!" was written over the portal of the antique world. Over the portal of the new world "Be thyself" shall be written. And the message of Christ to man was simply "Be thyself". That is the secret of Christ.

The Soul of Man under Socialism

The supreme vice is shallowness.

Letters

… the past is of no importance. The present is of no importance. It is with the future that we have to deal.

The Soul of Man under Socialism

… this age of ours, an age that reads so much that it has no time to admire, and writes so much that it has no time to think.

Letters

Modern life is complex and relative. Those are its two distinguishing notes. To render the first we require atmosphere with its subtlety of nuances, of suggestion, of strange perspectives; as for the second we require background. That is why Sculpture has ceased to be a representative art; and why Music is a representative art; and why Literature is, and has been, and always will remain the supreme representative art.

Letters

We call ourselves a utilitarian age, and we do not know the uses of any single thing. We have forgotten that Water can cleanse, and Fire purify, and that the Earth is mother to us all.

Letters

... it is only the modern that ever becomes old-fashioned ... M. Zola sits down to give us a picture of the Second Empire. Who cares for the Second Empire now? It is out of date. Life goes faster than Realism, but Romanticism is always in front of Life.

The Decay of Lying

Modern morality consists in accepting the standard of one's age ... for any man of culture to accept the standard of his age is a form of the grossest immorality.

The Picture of Dorian Gray

To me the mirror of perfect friendship can never be dulled by any treachery, however mean, or disloyalty, however base. Individuals come and go like shadows but the ideal remains untarnished always: the ideal of lives linked together not by affection merely, or the pleasantness of companionship, but by the capacity of being stirred by the same noble things in art and song ...

... friendship is a fire where what is not flawless shrinks into grey ashes, and where what is imperfect is not purified but consumed.

Letters

... there is no such thing as a romantic experience; there are romantic memories, and there is the desire of romance — that is all. Our most fiery moments of ecstasy are merely shadows of what somewhere else we have felt, or of what we long some day to feel ... I myself would sacrifice everything for a new experience, and I know there is no such thing as a new experience at all ... Only one thing remains infinitely fascinating to me, the mystery of moods. To be master of these moods is exquisite, to be mastered by them more exquisite still. Sometimes I think that the artistic life is a long and lovely suicide, and am not sorry that it is so.

Letters

Love is fed by the imagination, by which we become wiser than we know, better than we feel, nobler than we are: by which we can see Life as a whole ... Only what is fine can feed ... Love. But anything will feed hate.

Letters

[Of Jesus] Philistinism being simply that side of man's nature that is not illumined by the imagination, he sees all the lovely influences of life as modes of light: the imagination is the world-light … the world is made by it, and yet the world cannot understand it: that is because the imagination is simply a manifestation of Love, and it is love, and the capacity for it, that distinguishes one human being from another.

Letters

… Ay! without love
Life is no better than the unhewn stone
Which in the quarry lies, before the sculptor
Has set the God within it. Without love
Life is as silent as the common reeds
That through the marshes or by rivers grow,
And have no music in them.

The Duchess of Padua

Nothing should be out of the reach of hope. Life is a hope.

A Woman of No Importance

A map of the world that does not include Utopia is not worth even glancing at, for it leaves out the one country at which Humanity is always landing ... And ... looks out, and seeing a better country, sets sail. Progress is the realization of Utopias.

The Soul of Man under Socialism

                       ... Liberty!
For this sake only do thy dissonant cries
Delight my discreet soul, else might all kings
By bloody knout or treacherous cannonades
Rob nations of their rights inviolate
And I remain unmoved – and yet, and yet,
These Christs that die upon the barricades,
God knows it I am with them, in some things.

"Sonnet to Liberty"

Disobedience, in the eyes of anyone who has read history, is man's original virtue. It is through disobedience that progress has been made, through disobedience and through rebellion.

The Soul of Man under Socialism

Discontent is the first step in the progress of a man or a nation.

A Woman of No Importance

What is said by great employers of labour against agitators is unquestionably true. Agitators are a set of interfering, meddling people, who come down to some perfectly contented class of the community, and sow the seeds of discontent amongst them. That is the reason why agitators are so absolutely necessary.

The Soul of Man under Socialism

Slavery was put down in America, not in consequence of any action on the part of the slaves … It was put down entirely through the grossly illegal conduct of certain agitators in Boston and elsewhere, who were not slaves themselves, nor owners of slaves, nor had anything to do with the question really.

The Soul of Man under Socialism

… the most tragic fact in the whole of the French Revolution is not that Marie Antoinette was killed for being a queen, but that the starved peasant of the Vendée voluntarily went out to die for the hideous cause of feudalism.

The Soul of Man under Socialism

… charity degrades and demoralizes … Charity creates a multitude of sins.

The Soul of Man under Socialism

Of course, we have to a very great extent got rid of any attempt on the part of the community, or the Church, or the Government, to interfere with the individualism of speculative thought, but the attempt to interfere with the individualism of imaginative art still lingers. In fact, it does more than linger; it is aggressive, offensive and brutalizing.

The Soul of Man under Socialism

The majority of people spoil their lives by an unhealthy and exaggerated altruism … They find themselves surrounded by hideous poverty, by hideous ugliness, by hideous starvation. It is inevitable that they should be strongly moved by this. The emotions of man are stirred more quickly than man's intelligence … it is much more easy to have sympathy with suffering than it is to have sympathy with thought. Accordingly, with admirable, though misdirected intentions … they … set themselves to the task of remedying the evils that they see. But their remedies do not cure the disease: they merely prolong it. Indeed their remedies are part of the disease.

The Soul of Man under Socialism

But pity seems to beat in vain at the doors of offi-
cialism; and power, no less than punishment, kills
what else were good and gentle in a man ...

Letters

~❦~

The man had killed the thing he loved,
And so he had to die.

Yet each man kills the thing he loves,
By each let this be heard,
Some do it with a bitter look,
Some with a flattering word.
The coward does it with a kiss,
The brave man with a sword! ...

Some love too little, some too long,
Some sell, and others buy;
Some do the deed with many tears,
And some without a sigh:
For each man kills the thing he loves,
Yet each man does not die.

"The Ballad of Reading Gaol"

For Man's grim Justice goes its way,
And will not swerve aside:
It slays the weak, it slays the strong,
It has a deadly stride: ...

"The Ballad of Reading Gaol"

I know not whether Laws be right,
Or whether Laws be wrong;
All that we know who lie in gaol
Is that the wall is strong; ...

"The Ballad of Reading Gaol"

Ordinary cruelty is simply stupidity. It is the entire
want of imagination. It is the result in our days of
stereotyped systems of hard-and-fast rules, and of
stupidity. What is inhuman in modern life is offi-
cialism. Authority is as destructive to those who exercise it as to those on whom it is exercised.

Letters

If the Socialism is Authoritarian; if there are Governments armed with economic power as they are now with political power; if, in a word, we are to have Industrial Tyrannies, then the last state of man will be worse than the first.

The Soul of Man under Socialism

All modes of government are failures. Despotism is unjust to everybody, including the despot, who was probably made for better things. Oligarchies are unjust to the many, and ochlocracies [mob rule] are unjust to the few. High hopes were once formed of democracy; but democracy means simply the bludgeoning of the people by the people for the people.

The Soul of Man under Socialism

... all authority is quite degrading. It degrades those who exercise it, and degrades those over whom it is exercised. When it is violently, grossly, and cruelly used, it produces a good effect, by creating, or at any rate bringing out, the spirit of revolt ...

The Soul of Man under Socialism

Better the rule of One, whom all obey,
Than to let clamorous demagogues betray
Our freedom with the kiss of anarchy.
Wherefore I love them not whose hands profane
Plant the red flag upon the piled-up street
For no right cause, beneath whose ignorant reign
Arts, Culture, Reverence, Honour, all things fade,
Save Treason and the dagger of her trade,
And Murder with his silent bloody feet.

"Libertatis Sacra Fames"
[The holy hunger for freedom]

The form of government that is most suitable to the artist is no government at all.

The Soul of Man under Socialism

There are three kinds of despots. There is the despot who tyrannizes over the body. There is the despot who tyrannizes over the soul. There is the despot who tyrannizes over the body and soul alike. The first is called the Prince. The second is called the Pope. The third is called the People.

The Soul of Man under Socialism

… a community is infinitely more brutalized by the habitual employment of punishment than it is by the occasional occurrence of crime.

The Soul of Man under Socialism

"In war," answered the weaver, "the strong make slaves of the weak, and in peace the rich make slaves of the poor ... "

The Young King

It is immoral to use private property in order to alleviate the horrible evils that result from the institution of private property.

The Soul of Man under Socialism

If property had simply pleasures, we could stand it; but its duties make it unbearable. In the interest of the rich we must get rid of it. The virtues of the poor may be readily admitted, and are much to be regretted.

The Soul of Man under Socialism

... the recognition of private property has really harmed Individualism, and obscured it, by confusing a man with what he possesses.

The Soul of Man under Socialism

The true perfection of man lies, not in what man has, but in what man is.

The Soul of Man under Socialism

With the abolition of private property ... Nobody will waste his life in accumulating things, and the symbols for things. One will live. To live is the rarest thing in the world. Most people exist, that is all.

The Soul of Man under Socialism

There is only one class in the community that thinks more about money than the rich, and that is the poor. The poor can think of nothing else. That is the misery of being poor.

The Soul of Man under Socialism

To be entirely free, and at the same time entirely dominated by law, is the eternal paradox of human life …

Letters

… I like no law at all:
Were there no law there'd be no law-breakers,
So all men would be virtuous.

The Duchess of Padua

The gods are strange. It is not of our vices only they make instruments to scourge us. They bring us to ruin through what in us is good, gentle, humane, loving.

Letters

❧

… Prosperity, Pleasure and Success may be rough of grain and common in fibre, but … Sorrow is the most sensitive of all created things. There is nothing that stirs in the whole world of thought or motion to which Sorrow does not vibrate in terrible if exquisite pulsation.

Letters

❧

The poor are wiser, more charitable, more kind, more sensitive than we are. In their eyes prison is a tragedy in a man's life, a misfortune, a casualty, something that calls for sympathy in others.

Letters

Clergymen, and people who use phrases without wisdom, sometimes talk of suffering as a mystery. It is really a revelation. One discerns things that one never discerned before.

Letters

Pleasure for the beautiful body, but Pain for the beautiful Soul.

Letters

Most people are other people. Their thoughts are someone else's opinions, their life a mimicry, their passions a quotation.

Letters

[Of Jesus] Like all poetical natures, he loved ignorant people. He knew that in the soul of one who is ignorant there is always room for a great idea. But he could not stand stupid people, especially those who are made stupid by education – people who are full of opinions not one of which they can understand, a peculiarly modern type ... who has the key of knowledge, can't use it himself, and won't allow other people to use it.

Letters

Of course the sinner must repent. But why? Simply because otherwise he would be unable to realise what he had done. The moment of repentance is the moment of initiation.

Letters

Nobody can shift their responsibilities on anyone else. They always return ultimately to the proper owner.

Letters

The ugly and the stupid have the best of it in this world … If they know nothing of victory, they are at least spared the knowledge of defeat. They live as we all should live, undisturbed, indifferent, and without disquiet.

The Picture of Dorian Gray

Conscience and cowardice are really the same thing … Conscience is the trade-name of the firm. That is all.

The Picture of Dorian Gray

Conscience is but the name which cowardice
Fleeing from battle scrawls upon its shield.

The Duchess of Padua

All influence is immoral – immoral from the scientific point of view … Because to influence a person is to give him one's own soul. He does not think his natural thoughts or burn with his natural passions.

The Picture of Dorian Gray

Nothing can cure the soul but the senses, just as nothing can cure the senses but the soul.

The Picture of Dorian Gray

I wonder who it was who defined man as a rational animal. It was the most premature definition ever given. Man is many things, but he is not rational.

The Picture of Dorian Gray

The reason we all like to think so well of others is that we are all afraid for ourselves. The basis of optimism is sheer terror. We think that we are generous because we credit our neighbour with the possession of those virtues that are likely to be a benefit to us. We praise the banker that we may overdraw our account, and find good qualities in the highwayman in the hope that he may spare our pockets.

The Picture of Dorian Gray

Pleasure is Nature's test, her sign of approval. When we are happy we are always good, but when we are good we are not always happy.

The Picture of Dorian Gray

We can have in life but one great experience at best, and the secret of life is to reproduce that experience as often as possible.

The Picture of Dorian Gray

If one puts forward an idea to a true Englishman –
always a rash thing to do – he never dreams of considering whether the idea is right or wrong. The only
thing he considers of any importance is whether one
believes it oneself. Now, the value of an idea has
nothing to do with the sincerity of the man who
expresses it. Indeed the probabilities are that the more
insincere the man is, the more purely intellectual will
the idea be, as in that case it will not be coloured by
either his wants, his desires, or his prejudices.

The Portrait of Mr W. H.

… to recommend thrift to the poor is both grotesque
and insulting. It is like advising a man who is starving
to eat less.

The Soul of Man under Socialism

As for the virtuous poor, one can pity them of course, but one cannot possibly admire them. They have made private terms with the enemy, and sold their birthright for very bad pottage.

The Soul of Man under Socialism

Misery and poverty are so absolutely degrading, and exercise such a paralysing effect over the nature of men, that no class is ever really conscious of its own suffering.

The Soul of Man under Socialism

… a great deal of nonsense is being written and talked nowadays about the dignity of manual labour. There is nothing necessarily dignified about manual labour at all, and most of it is absolutely degrading.

The Soul of Man under Socialism

... man has been ... the slave of machinery ... At present machinery competes against man. Under proper conditions machinery will serve man.

The Soul of Man under Socialism

The fact is, that civilization requires slaves. The Greeks were quite right there ... Human slavery is wrong, insecure, and demoralizing. On mechanical slavery, on the slavery of the machine, the future of the world depends.

The Soul of Man under Socialism

... whenever a community ... attempts to dictate to the artist what he is to do, Art either entirely vanishes, or becomes stereotyped, or degenerates into a low and ignoble form of craft.

The Soul of Man under Socialism

… Public Opinion … bad and well-meaning as it is when it tries to control action, is infamous and of evil meaning when it tries to control Thought or Art.

The Soul of Man under Socialism

The one thing that the public dislike is novelty … because they are afraid of it.

The Soul of Man under Socialism

The private lives of men and women should not be told to the public. The public have nothing to do with them at all.

The Soul of Man under Socialism

... better to stand aloof
Far from these slanderous fools who mock my life
Knowing me not, better the lowliest roof
Fit for the meanest hind to sojourn in,
Than to go back to that hoarse cave of strife
Where my white soul first kissed the mouth of sin.

                                    "Taedium Vitae"

It is to be noted that Individualism does not come to the man with any sickly cant about duty, which merely means doing what other people want because they want it.

The Soul of Man under Socialism

We are each our own devil, and we make
This world our hell ...

                        The Duchess of Padua

The ages live in history through their anachronisms.
    "Phrases and Philosophies for the Use of the Young"

Industry is the root of all ugliness.
    "Phrases and Philosophies for the Use of the Young"

If a man needs an elaborate tombstone in order to remain in the memory of his country, it is clear that his living at all was an act of absolute superfluity.

Letters

Work never seems to me a reality, but a way of getting rid of reality.

Letters

The growth of common sense in the English Church is a thing very much to be regretted. It is really a degrading concession to a low form of realism. It is silly, too. It springs from an entire ignorance of psychology. Man can believe the impossible, but man can never believe the improbable.

The Decay of Lying

The chief advantage that would result from the establishment of Socialism is, undoubtedly, the fact that Socialism would relieve us from that sordid necessity of living for others which, in the present condition of things, presses so hardly upon almost everybody. In fact, scarcely anyone at all escapes.

The Soul of Man under Socialism

… the worst slave-owners were those who were kind to their slaves, and so prevented the horror of the system being realized by those who suffered from it, and understood by those who contemplated it.

The Soul of Man under Socialism

I don't think now that people can be divided into the good and the bad as though they were two separate races of creation.

Lady Windermere's Fan

～⧊～

There is the same world for all of us, and good and evil, sin and innocence, go through it hand in hand. To shut one's eyes to half of life that one may live securely is as though one blinded oneself that one might walk with more safety in a land of pit and precipice.

Lady Windermere's Fan

～⧊～

It has been pointed out that one of the results of the extraordinary tyranny of authority is that words are absolutely distorted from their proper and simple meaning, and are used to express the obverse of their right signification.

The Soul of Man under Socialism

Oh, your English society seems to me shallow, selfish, foolish. It has blinded its eyes, and stopped its ears. It lies like a leper in purple. It sits like a dead thing smeared with gold. It is all wrong, all wrong.

A Woman of No Importance

HESTER: Lord Henry Watson! I remember him ... A man with a hideous smile and a hideous past. He is asked everywhere. No dinner-party is complete without him. What of those whose ruin is due to him? They are outcasts. They are nameless. If you met them in the street you would turn your head away.

A Woman of No Importance

If a man and woman have sinned, let them both go forth into the desert to love or loathe each other there. Let them both be branded ... but don't punish the one and let the other go free. Don't have one law for men and another for women. You are unjust to women in England. And till you count what is a shame in a woman to be an infamy in a man, you will always be unjust, and Right, that pillar of fire, and Wrong, that pillar of cloud, will be made dim to your eyes, or not be seen at all, or if seen, not regarded.

A Woman of No Importance

When a man is old enough to do wrong he should be old enough to do right also.

A Woman of No Importance

There are other countries than England ... Oh! other countries over sea, better, wiser, and less unjust lands.

A Woman of No Importance

Hearts live by being wounded. Pleasure may turn a heart to stone, riches may make it callous, but sorrow – oh, sorrow cannot break it.

A Woman of No Importance

In old days nobody pretended to be a bit better than his neighbours. In fact, to be a bit better than one's neighbour was considered excessively vulgar and middle-class. Nowadays, with our modern mania for morality, everyone has to pose as a paragon of purity, incorruptibility, and all the other seven deadly virtues – and what is the result? You all go over like ninepins … Not a year passes in England without somebody disappearing. Scandals used to lend charm, or at least interest to a man – now they crush him.

An Ideal Husband

One's past is what one is. It is the only way by which people should be judged.

An Ideal Husband

It is when we are wounded by our own hands, or by the hands of others, that love should come to cure us — else what use is love at all? All sins, except a sin against itself, Love should forgive.

An Ideal Husband

Slander and folly have their way for a season, but for a season only ...

Letters

Who are these scribes who, passing from crime to criticism, sway with such serene incapacity the office which they so lately swept? "Narcissuses of imbecility," what should they see in the clear waters of Beauty and in the well undefiled of Truth but the shifting and shadowy image of their own substantial stupidity? Secure of that oblivion for which they toil so laboriously and, I must acknowledge, with such success, let them peer at us through their telescopes and report what they like of us. But ... should we put them under the microscope there would be really nothing to be seen.

Letters

All good plays are a combination of the dream of a poet and that practical knowledge of the actor which gives concentration to action, which intensifies situation, and for poetic effect, which is description, substitutes dramatic effect, which is Life.

Letters

Now, one of the facts of physiology is the desire of any very intensified emotion to be relieved by some emotion that is its opposite. Nature's example of dramatic effect is the laughter of hysteria or the tears of joy.

Letters

The present style of burying and sorrowing for the dead seems to me to make grief grotesque, and to turn mourning to a mockery … The ceremony by which we part from those whom we have loved should not merely be noble in its meaning, but simple in its sincerity.

Letters

Bother space and time! They spoil life by allowing such a thing as distance.

Letters

There is something so unique about Christ. Of course, just as there are false dawns before the dawn itself, and winter-days so full of sudden sunlight that they will cheat the wise crocus into squandering its gold before its time, and make some foolish bird call to its mate to build on barren boughs, so there were Christians before Christ. For that we should be grateful. The unfortunate thing is that there have been none since.

Letters

People point to Reading Gaol, and say "There is where the artistic life leads a man." Well, it might lead one to worse places. The more mechanical people, to whom life is a shrewd speculation dependent on a careful calculation of ways and means, always know where they are going, and go there. They start with the desire of being the Parish Beadle, and, in whatever sphere they are placed, they succeed in being the Parish Beadle and no more. A man whose desire is to be something separate from himself, to be a Member of Parliament, or a successful grocer, or a prominent solicitor, or a judge, or something equally tedious, invariably succeeds in being what he wants to be. That is his punishment. Those who want a mask have to wear it.

Letters

But to recognize that the soul of man is unknowable is the ultimate achievement of Wisdom. The final mystery is oneself. When one has weighed the sun in a balance, and measured the steps of the moon, and mapped out the seven heavens star by star, there still remains oneself. Who can calculate the orbit of his own soul?

Letters

Things in themselves are of little importance, have indeed — let us for once thank Metaphysics for something that she has taught us — no real existence. The spirit alone is of importance.

Letters

But there is nothing in the world so wrong but that the spirit of Humanity, which is the spirit of Love, the spirit of the Christ who is not in Churches, may make it, if not right, at least possible to be borne without too much bitterness of heart.

Letters

I need not tell you that to me Reformations in Morals are as meaningless and vulgar as Reformations in Theology. But while to propose to be a better man is a piece of unscientific cant, to have become a deeper man is the privilege of those who have suffered.

Letters

I have a right to share in Sorrow, and he who can look at the loveliness of the world, and share its sorrow, and realize something of the wonder of both, is in immediate contact with divine things, and has got as near to God's secret as anyone can get.

Letters

And delightful as cynicism is from its intellectual side, now that it has left the Tub for the Club, it never can be more than the perfect philosophy for a man who has no soul. It has its social value, and to an artist all modes of expression are interesting, but in itself is a poor affair, for to the true cynic nothing is ever revealed.

Letters

Emotional forces ... are as limited in extent and duration as the forces of physical energy. The little cup that is made to hold so much can hold so much and no more, though all the purple vats of Burgundy be filled with wine to the brim, and the treaders stand knee-deep in the gathered grapes of the stony vine-yards of Spain. There is no error more common than that of thinking that those who are the causes of occa-sions of great tragedies share in the feelings suitable to the tragic mood: no error more fatal than expecting it of them. The martyr in his "shirt of flame" may be looking on the face of God, but to him who is piling the faggots or loosening the logs for the blast the whole scene is no more than the slaying of an ox is to the butcher, or the felling of a tree to the charcoal-burner in the forest, or the fall of a flower to one who is mowing down the grass with a scythe. Great passions are for the great of soul, and great events can be seen only by those who are on a level with them.

Letters

Remember that imagination is the quality that enables one to see things and people in their real as in their ideal relations.

Letters

Do not be afraid of the past. If people tell you it is irrevocable, do not believe them. The past, the present and the future are but one moment in the sight of God, in whose sight we should try to live. Time and space, succession and extension, are merely accidental conditions of Thought. The Imagination can transcend them, and move in a free sphere of ideal existences. Things, also, are in their essence what we choose to make them. A thing is, according to the mode in which one looks at it.

Letters

Life is not complex. We are complex. Life is simple, and the simple thing is the right thing.

Letters

Only the imagination of man is limitless. The appetite seems curiously bounded. This is one of the many lessons I have learnt.

Letters

I used to think gratitude a heavy burden for one to carry. Now I know that it is something that makes the heart lighter. The ungrateful man seems to me to be one who walks with feet and heart of lead. But when one has learnt, however inadequately, what a lovely thing gratitude is, one's feet go lightly over sand or sea, and one finds a strange joy revealed to one, the joy of counting up not what one possesses, but what one owes.

Letters

The gift of prophecy is given to all those who do not know what is going to happen to themselves.

Letters

Love can canonize people. The saints are those who have been most loved.

Letters

… personality does not require intellect to help it: it is a dynamic force of its own, and is often as superbly unintelligent as the great forces of nature …

Letters

Nemesis has caught me in her net: to struggle is foolish. Why is it that one runs to one's ruin? Why has destruction such a fascination? Why, when one stands on a pinnacle, must one throw oneself down? No one knows, but things are so.

Letters

I cannot live without the atmosphere of Love: I must love and be loved, whatever price I pay for it.

Letters

In point of fact, describing a prison is as difficult artistically as describing a water-closet would be. If one had to describe the latter in literature, prose or verse, one could merely say it was well, or badly, papered: or clean or the reverse: the horror of prison is that everything is so simple and commonplace in itself, and so degrading, and hideous, and revolting in its effect.

Letters

I never came across anyone in whom the moral sense was dominant who was not heartless, cruel, vindictive, log-stupid, and entirely lacking in the smallest sense of humanity. Moral people, as they are termed, are simple beasts. I would sooner have fifty unnatural vices than one unnatural virtue. It is unnatural virtue that makes the world, for those who suffer, such a premature Hell.

Letters

Christ did not die to save people, but to teach people how to save each other.

Letters

There is a fatality about all physical and intellectual distinction, the sort of fatality that seems to dog through history the faltering steps of kings. It is better not to be different from one's fellows.

The Picture of Dorian Gray

Laughter is not at all a bad beginning for a friendship, and it is far the best ending for one.

The Picture of Dorian Gray

The harmony of soul and body — how much that is! We in our madness have separated the two, and have invented a realism that is vulgar, an ideality that is void.

The Picture of Dorian Gray

The terror of society, which is the basis of morals, the terror of God, which is the secret of religion – these are the two things that govern us.

The Picture of Dorian Gray

Humanity takes itself too seriously. It is the world's original sin. If the caveman had known how to laugh, History would have been different.

The Picture of Dorian Gray

As it was, we always misunderstood ourselves and rarely understood others.

The Picture of Dorian Gray

There is a luxury in self-reproach. When we blame ourselves we feel that no one else has a right to blame us.

The Picture of Dorian Gray

It often happens that the real tragedies of life occur in such an inartistic manner that they hurt us by their crude violence, their absolute incoherence, their absurd want of meaning, their entire lack of style. They affect us just as vulgarity affects us. They give us an impression of sheer brute force, and we revolt against that. Sometimes, however, a tragedy that possesses artistic elements of beauty crosses our lives. If these elements of beauty are real, the whole thing simply appeals to our sense of dramatic effect. Suddenly we find that we are no longer the actors, but the spectators of the play. Or rather we are both. We watch ourselves, and the mere wonder of the spectacle enthrals us.

The Picture of Dorian Gray

The worship of the senses has often, and with much justice, been decried, men feeling a natural instinct of terror about passions and sensations that seem stronger than themselves, and that they are conscious of sharing with the less highly organized forms of existence.

The Picture of Dorian Gray

But he never fell into the error of arresting his intellectual development by any formal acceptance of
creed or system, or of mistaking, for a house in which
to live, an inn that is but suitable for the sojourn of a
night ...

The Picture of Dorian Gray

For the canons of good society are, or should be, the
same as the canons of art. Form is absolutely essential
to it. It should have the dignity of a ceremony, as well
as its unreality, and should combine the insincere
character of a romantic play with the wit and beauty
that make such plays delightful to us. Is insincerity
such a terrible thing? I think not. It is merely a
method by which we can multiply our personalities.

The Picture of Dorian Gray

Sin is a thing that writes itself across a man's face. It cannot be concealed. People talk sometimes of secret vices. There are no such things. If a wretched man has a vice, it shows itself in the lines of his mouth, the droop of his eyelids, the moulding of his hands even.

The Picture of Dorian Gray

Each man lived his own life, and paid his own price for living it. The only pity was one had to pay so often for a single fault. One had to pay over and over again, indeed. In her dealings with man Destiny never closed her accounts.

The Picture of Dorian Gray

There are moments, psychologists tell us, when the passion for sin, or for what the world calls sin, so dominates a nature, that every fibre of the body, as every cell of the brain, seems to be instinct with fearful impulses. Men and women at such moments lose the freedom of their will. They move to their terrible end as automatons move. Choice is taken from them, and conscience is either killed, or, if it lives at all, lives but to give rebellion its fascination, and disobedience its charm.

The Picture of Dorian Gray

Actual life was chaos, but there was something terribly logical in the imagination. It was the imagination that set remorse to dog the feet of sin. It was the imagination that made each crime bear its misshapen brood. In the common world of fact the wicked were not punished, nor the good rewarded. Success was given to the strong, failure thrust upon the weak. That was all.

The Picture of Dorian Gray